Elizabeth Blackwell

THE BARNARD BIOGRAPHY SERIES

Elizabeth Blackwell

A Doctor's Triumph

Nancy Kline

Foreword by Nancy Neveloff Dubler

CONARI PRESS
Berkeley, California

Conari Press books are distributed by Publishers Group West

Cover design: Suzanne Albertson
Cover portrait: Lino Saffioti
Illustration credit, page xvii: Charles Pfizer & Company

ISBN: 1-57324-057-5

Library of Congress Cataloging-in-Publication Data
Kline, Nancy.
    Elizabeth Blackwell: a doctor's triumph / by Nancy Kline;
foreword by Nancy Dubler.
        p.   cm. — (A Barnard Biography Series; 2)
        Includes bibliographical references and index.
        Summary: Describes the personal life and achievements of
the woman credited with being the first woman physician in
the United States.
        ISBN 1-57324-057-5 (trade paper)
        1. Blackwell, Elizabeth, 1821–1910—Juvenile literature.
    2. Women physicians—United States—Biography—Juvenile
literature. [1. Blackwell, Elizabeth, 1821–1910. 2. Physicians.
3. Women—Biography.]   I. Title.   II. Series: Barnard biography series (Berkeley, Calif.); 2.

    R154.B623K576   1997
    610'3.92—dc20
    [B]   96–42011
                                                CIP
                                                AC

Printed in the United States of America on recycled paper
10 9 8 7 6 5 4 3 2 1

*For
Adam
and
Ana*

Acknowledgments

A number of people have given this biography attentive readings and have offered invaluable suggestions as to how it might be strengthened. I want to thank them all. Among my earliest and most helpful audiences were the XIs, XIIs, and XIIIs of City & Country School and their teacher Ellen Wertzel, as well as the members of the Women Writing Women's Lives Seminar. Both Theresa Rogers and Nancy Woloch of Barnard College read the book with an expert eye and made detailed and insightful comments on the manuscript that were crucial to its revision.

I am grateful to Sandra and Kelly Turner for their enthusiasm, support, and patience in the early stages of the project; to Dr. Ann Yee and Dr. Morris Podolsky for their technical expertise; and to the Virginia Center for the Creative Arts and The MacDowell Colony for providing me with the space and silence in which to finish my work.

Special thanks are due Catherine Gourley, my exemplary editor at Conari Press, for the scrupulous attention with which she read and helped to shape the manuscript, and for her grace and humor in dealing with its author.

To Beverly Solochek, who championed the book from the very start, I offer my deepest gratitude. She is a splendid colleague and a dear friend.

Contents

Foreword

Twenty years ago, when my daughter was four, her post nursery school treats included watching *Sesame Street*. In one particular episode, the Cookie Monster was visited by a doctor—a woman—who prescribed medicine for his fever. My daughter seemed puzzled. Men were doctors, she explained confidently, and women were nurses. She delivered this review of gender divisions in the healing professions despite the fact that she was regularly cared for by a woman pediatrician, her teeth examined by a woman dentist, and her eyes tested by a woman ophthalmologist. Six months before, when her brother had mashed her finger in the hinge of the door, she had been sutured by a woman surgeon. Despite personal history, however, her observations reflected both the power of popular imagery and how slowly masculine professional hegemony in medicine had receded.

Elizabeth Blackwell, the first woman doctor in America, had begun the process of professional reform in 1847, when she was admitted to the Geneva Medical College of Western Medicine on a fluke. For Elizabeth, entrance into medical school was the result of years of dogged persistence in pursuit of her dream to become a doctor.

The reasons for the exclusion of women from the professions were many. Acceptable eighteenth century notions of middle-class womanhood began and ended with domesticity. Lower-class women and girls regularly worked at bone-crunching jobs, acting as donkeys and pulling carts in the coal mines or toiling in the factories for long days and a few pennies' wages, but middle-class women were restricted to work in the home, cultivating delicate sensibilities and house-womanly skills and virtues. Victorian sensibilities, values, and laws precluded women's independence and suffrage, most inheritance, and all professional learning and opportunity.

Victorian prudishness also recoiled at the notion of a woman learning about or touching a body. Medicine was about bodies, and bodies were shameful aspects of the human condition to be denied and hidden away. Discussions about body functions, illness, disease, and sexuality were not proper in any polite company that included women.

Not only did the biases of society differ from our own, but the practice of medicine would be unrecognizable to a contemporary physician. In Elizabeth Blackwell's time, medicine would occasionally diagnose, sometimes give comfort, but almost never cure. Surgery was done without anesthesia, and many patients preferred certain death to the horror of the surgical knife. Antisepsis was unknown and physicians went from one patient to another spreading the very diseases they sought to combat. The discovery of antibiotics was still a century away, and the development of machines to support breathing, heart rhythms, and kidney function were not even within the purview of futuristic speculation.

What medicine was, however, was a large and fairly well-organized men's club that offered some prestige and—for at least some doctors—substantial financial reward. There was no state licensing of physicians and anyone who chose to could post a sign and begin practice. Some had skill and education; others had little more than callous disregard for the welfare of the patient.

The worst care was probably that given to women. Victorian prudishness banned male physicians from looking at their female patients if they were examining them for vaginal or uterine illness or for breast cancer. A broken ankle might be carefully examined but little else was. Women escaped total butchery because childbirth was largely handled by women midwives whose formal education, folk wisdom, and empathy prepared them—somewhat—to assist during childbirth with at least a small modicum of competence. But this, too, was under attack as physicians, seeing midwives as competitors, tried to have laws passed that would prohibit non-physicians from supervising childbirth.

In Elizabeth Blackwell's time, various states first began to pass statutes that made abortion a crime. For some men, who were then the sole occupants of state legislatures, these statutes reflected religious dictate and moral obligation; for others, they were the means to limit women's decision-making ability over family size and to restrict the place of women in medicine. As midwifery was strangled, it left the care of women in the hands of men.

In Elizabeth Blackwell's time, a woman's individual choices about careers, about the size and timing of a family, and about how women can control their own bodies were denied. Rather than accepting the way things were, Elizabeth Blackwell responded to this powerlessness. Determined to change the complex economic, social, and moral universe that was her world, Elizabeth Blackwell provided women with skilled and sensitive care so that they would not choose death over the horrible prospect of being touched or examined by a strange man.

Elizabeth Blackwell's successful completion of medical school, supported by her peers and a few sympathetic professors, was followed by unsuccessful attempts to continue her postgraduate medical education in hospitals in the United States. As a result, she continued her postgraduate medical education in England and France. Despite these handicaps and the restrictions of her time, Blackwell's accomplishments were formidable. With her sister Emily and a young German midwife whom she helped to train in medicine, she established a medical practice and set up a clinic for the poor. By the end of the Civil War in 1865, the clinic was treating 7,000 patients a year. In 1868, the Infirmary had spawned the Woman's Medical College of the New York Infirmary.

Elizabeth Blackwell's story tells much more than how one woman struggled to become a respected doctor. Her story is about the education and care of women and of all medical patients. Her work continues today. As Nancy Kline notes in this biography, despite Elizabeth Blackwell's success, women students represented a very small percent of medical school enrollment through the end of the nineteenth and through half of the twentieth century. Not until the women's rights revolution of the 1960s did women enroll in medical school in any great number.

Now thirty years later, women comprise 50 percent of most medical school enrollment. But the work on women's health issues remains important and underexplored. Women of color and adolescents now make up the fastest growing populations in the epidemic of AIDS. Many poor women live in areas with a high prevalence of HIV infection and are at risk for the transmission of the disease in any sexual encounter where a condom is not used. Yet many women do not have the power in a relationship to insist on "safer" sex.

The National Institutes of Health, that branch of the government that oversees medical research and provides funds for specific research projects, set up the first Office for Women's Health in 1993 and only now is insisting that women be included. The right of a woman to control her body and to choose an abortion remains protected by the courts but is constantly under attack. And many women who want to exercise that right find that there is no doctor in their locality who is trained in doing abortions and willing to do so.

A young child today might not be surprised to see the Cookie Monster being treated by a woman doctor. The imagery of doctors has changed dramatically since my own daughter was a child. But the women's revolution in health care continues. Nancy Kline relates that shortly after Elizabeth Blackwell's success in entering a medical school was reported in the media, a woman applied to the prestigious Harvard Medical School and was promptly rejected.

Almost a century and a half later, I entered the Harvard Law School in only the fourteenth class that had admitted women, at a time when professors were unembarrassed at targeting women as butts of class humor. Elizabeth Blackwell helped to pave the way for women in the professions. From her struggles, our lives may be more fulfilled.

Nancy Neveloff Dubler

Nancy Neveloff Dubler, who received her A.B. from Barnard College in 1964 and her L.L.B. from Harvard Law School in 1967, is one of the nation's leading bioethicists. Director of the Division of Bioethics at Montefiore Medical Center and Professor of Bioethics at Albert Einstein College of Medicine in the Bronx, New York, she lectures and writes extensively on topics such as the termination of care, geriatrics, AIDS, and home care.

Chapter One

One afternoon in 1859, Dr. Elizabeth Blackwell returned to visit the first house she remembered living in as a child, in the city of Bristol, England. She found the house, still standing on Wilson Street, much smaller than she had remembered it. And as she gazed around the high-ceilinged entryway, she suddenly seemed to see herself much smaller too, herself as a young child. Above her in the hall—just there—her own small childish face seemed to be peering wistfully over the banister, and the memory of a scene from her earliest childhood suddenly rose up around her.

All the others were downstairs in the dining room, talking and laughing and eating, while Mr. Burnet, a flamboyant Irishman from Cork, hilariously held forth. Of all the visitors who came to dinner at the Blackwell house—Christian missionaries like himself, philanthropists, social reformers, travelers freighted with tales—Mr. Burnet was the most compelling storyteller, the most uproarious commentator on the world and his own adventures in it. He had the Irish gift of gab. The little girl Elizabeth longed to listen to him, perched beside her older sisters at the children's table where they sat on festive occasions like this, enchanted witnesses to other people's lives out in the great wide world beyond the familiar house and the sugar refinery attached to it that constituted the universe they knew. But in her exile upstairs, all Elizabeth could hear was a distant burst of merriment each time the servants opened the dining room door to clear away the dishes or to carry in the next course.

She was being punished that evening for some sin, some childish piece of misbehavior. Her name had been written carefully into The Black Book carried everywhere by her Aunt Bar, who kept track of the children's failings and determined the appropriate punishment. She had sentenced Elizabeth to exclusion from tonight's party. Upstairs it was lonely—dark and silent except for the occasional scrabbling of night creatures under the eaves. It hurt to be shut out, it was enraging; and Elizabeth was filled with guilt at having been wicked enough to get her name into The Black Book. It would not happen again, she vowed.

Forty years later, standing in the familiar entryway, Elizabeth could not remember the specific mischief for which she had been blamed, but she would always remember the punishment. Nor would she forget how unquestioningly she had accepted it. Aunt Bar was a grown-up; she must be right: "I always accepted, without thought of resistance the decrees of my superiors," Elizabeth wrote years later. "The fact that those in authority were capable of injustice or stupidity was a perception of later growth."

During that same visit to the house on Wilson Street,

as she stood pondering the image of herself as a tiny child excluded, something truly startling happened. She heard the front door latch lift, clicking in the lock. She turned. Suddenly, there stood Papa Blackwell—who had been dead for many years—smiling directly at her, in the white flannel suit he used to wear during the hottest summer months when he went to work in his sugar house. And then he was gone. He seemed to leave behind the sweet and cloying scent of sugarcane.

Elizabeth Blackwell first arrived in Bristol on February 3, 1821. She was the fourth baby born to Hannah and Samuel Blackwell, and she was so puny that her parents doubted she would live. They had lost a baby son the year before, and now they watched this new baby daughter's struggle. They feared for her, such a tiny helpless thing. She seemed about to die.

But Elizabeth survived. She had been given her life, however tenuously, and she took hold of it and held on tight.

At the end of many days of watchfulness, when finally they felt sure that she had really come to stay, Hannah and Samuel called her two older sisters into the bedroom. One at a time, one rung at a time, five-year-old Anna and then three-year-old Marian clambered up the mahogany ladder at the side of Hannah Blackwell's high canopied bed and stared at their new sister. They laughed. They said her name. They welcomed her.

From the very first day, the runt of the litter never grew taller than five foot one. As a child, Elizabeth looked much more frail and vulnerable than her siblings. Her two older sisters, like their dark, high-spirited mother, were curly-haired brunettes, whereas Elizabeth took after her father, gray-eyed and somewhat grave, her blond hair straight and pale almost to invisibility. From the very first, "Little Shy," as her father quickly nicknamed her, was Papa's child. Elizabeth resembled him in more than simply physical ways. From him she took her stern perfectionism and her straight-faced wit and her obstinacy. As the Blackwell family grew and she came to have six younger siblings as well as two older sisters, Elizabeth proved to be more stubborn than all the rest of them put together, making up in sheer tenacity what she lacked in size. From the beginning, Little Shy sank her teeth so deeply and so doggedly into whatever it was she wanted that no one could shake her loose.

Her sisters and her brothers knew this about her. If there was something she couldn't do—a game she did not play as well as her brothers, a book that was too hard for her, a problem in arithmetic she could not solve—she kept on trying till she mastered it. The family knew it took her longer to get dressed than everybody else because she was so meticulous. And in those days there was so much for girls to get dressed in: in summertime, flowery frocks with puff sleeves tied with matching ribbons; in wintertime, dark worsted dresses worn beneath a pelisse; all this over pantalets and petticoats; and, on her feet, corked clogs or noisy wood-soled shoes or, if there was company coming, red slippers with crisscross ribbons.

Her family saw how her perfectionism was turned inward also. It wasn't just the outside world she wished to

4

conquer, but the world within her. Little Shy was always testing herself, trying to strengthen herself, "fighting the devil," as she called it. In imitation of the saints, she slept on the floor of her room, until her parents made her stop. She fasted during meals. When she had to give this up because it made her faint at the dinner table, she consented to eat, but turned down all her favorite foods. She hated being sick; it made her feel that her body was in control of her. Once when she was suffering from severe chills and fever, she refused to go to bed and tried to cure herself by walking them off (which didn't work). She seemed, even as a very little girl, to be perpetually honing her will. One day when she was only six years old, trailing after her two older sisters as they discussed what they wanted to be when they grew up, Elizabeth interjected: "I don't know what I'm going to be, but it will be something hard."

This purposeful, skinny child set her own uncompromising standards very early, scrambling along on the edge of other people's conversations, just the slightest bit excluded. She was, after all, the youngest of the three oldest Blackwell girls. She was always grouped with her two older sisters, but she was always, by definition, the third wheel—a six year old trying to keep up with a nine year old and an eleven year old. It meant she must aim higher. It reinforced the fact that she was somehow different, odd girl out—an impression underscored by the fact that the brother who was born right before her died, and the brother who was born right after her died. In later years, she spoke of her brothers and sisters as having come "all in twos": Anna and Marian, Samuel and Henry, Emily and

Ellen, Howard and George. Elizabeth saw herself as the cheese who stood alone, bracketed on either side by her dead brothers, separated from the rest of her family by just that much space, time, and death. A loner.

In fact, her mother gave birth thirteen times; two other children died in infancy as well. Elizabeth said later that she could scarcely remember a moment during her childhood when Mama was not either expecting or nursing a baby. But if this maternal image led to Elizabeth's future reverence for motherhood, as she said it did, the grown-up to whom she felt closest during all these crowded years was Papa. How she loved him. He made her laugh. He expected a great deal of her—as much as she herself did—and he was strict in bringing up his children, as strict as his three unmarried sisters who lived with the family. If he was tough, however, Samuel Blackwell also had a sense of humor, especially when turning down what he considered to be extravagant requests from his children. These they would submit to him in writing, and he would write back his reply ("No!") in the form of a verse.

One day, Elizabeth and her two older sisters had submitted a petition to him, asking that they be allowed to climb out on the roof so that they could see farther with Anna's new telescope. Her father responded:

> *Anna, Bessie, and Polly,*
> *   Your request is mere folly*
> *The leads are too high*
> *   For those who can't fly*
> *If I let you go there,*

I suppose your next prayer
Will be for a hop
 To the chimney top!
So I charge you three misses,
 Not to show your phizes
On parapet wall, or chimney so tall,
 But to keep on the earth,
The place of your birth.
 "Even so," says Papa. "Amen," says Mama.
"Be it so," says Aunt Bar.

Another time, when a cousin was to stay overnight, the three oldest Blackwell girls requested that all four of them be allowed to sleep in the enormous bed in the guest room. This was Papa's answer:

If you four little girls were together to lie,
I fear you'd resemble the pigs in their sty!
Such groaning! Such grunting! Such sprawling about!
I could not allow such confusion and rout! ! ! ! !
So this is my judgment: —'tis wisdom you'll own,
Two beds for four girls are far better than one!

His poetry, his warmth, his humor made Papa seem a "beneficent Providence" to Little Shy. She thought of him as a kind of god: witty, loving—and superhumanly demanding. His expectations of his family equaled his expectations of the rest of humanity. He dreamed of the possibility of a better world. He believed (as would his children after him) in the perfectibility of the human race. While this is admirable and inspiring, it is not

7

always easy to live with. Elizabeth's sister Anna characterized him as "excellent, most generous and affectionate," but spoke too of his "coldness of manner and austerity of ideas."

Samuel and his wife, Hannah, were strict Methodists. They believed that you were responsible, always, for your every action in this world. Each morning Samuel gathered his family and servants together for what Anna called a "horrid" reading of chapters from the Bible, followed by endless prayers, "the infliction [being] made before breakfast." Unlike Anna, Elizabeth enjoyed these daily prayer sessions, as she enjoyed Sundays, when the whole family attended morning and afternoon services at Bridge Street Chapel and spent the rest of the day learning hymns and biblical passages. Sometimes she even got to accompany Papa, who was a lay preacher, as he traveled through the countryside, delivering sermons.

The biggest social event in the Blackwell family calendar was missionary week, mid-May of every year, when everyone went to chapel every day, supplied with vast picnic lunches. They spent long hours listening, fascinated, to the exotic stories brought back to Bristol by returning missionaries.

Theirs was a household steeped in religion, and with it, hand-in-hand, went a belief in social reform. The Blackwells wanted to change the world. Papa worked for more democratic voting laws at a time and in a country where it was not only women but also the majority of men who were not allowed to vote. Only rich and privileged males had suffrage. He supported educational reform and equal rights for women. He preached temperance (total abstinence from drinking), and he was anti-slavery, despite the fact that he was a sugar refiner and both his city and his business were deeply intertwined with the slave trade.

Until 1807, when buying and selling slaves was outlawed in England, Bristol was a major slave-trading port, and in the ensuing years many of Samuel's colleagues continued to smuggle slaves to the colonies. There, they picked the sugarcane that was shipped to England to be refined into sugar. Samuel wrestled increasingly with the painful contradiction that he both opposed slavery and depended on it, a contradiction most clearly expressed by his own children the year they voluntarily gave up eating sugar (which paid their bills) since it was a "slave product."

Elizabeth was marked for life by her father's struggle and by her early exposure to evangelical Christianity and the social reform movement. The very same authority figure who ruled her childhood like a "beneficent Providence" also taught her to question authority, to rebel; and it was from Papa, too, that she learned the high cost of rebellion.

The Blackwells were not in danger of being jailed or killed for their beliefs, as were their forerunners, the Puritans. But their view of the world—that slavery was wrong and men and women might live as equals—was definitely a minority view, and especially as religious Dissenters, they were second-class citizens. In England during the 1820s, Dissenters were not permitted to hold the highest government offices. They could not work as doctors, lawyers, or professors. They were not allowed to study at British universities. They could not attend most lower schools. This was part of the reason why Elizabeth and her brothers and sisters did not go to school with other children, but studied instead with each other at home. As it happens, they got a better education that way, for Papa was particular about the governesses and tutors he employed. But the children's education, like their parents' politics and religion, isolated them from others.

The Blackwell family formed its own vigorous but nevertheless cut-off community. They remained somewhat apart, always partially turned in upon themselves, existing on the margins, separate.

Elizabeth spent the earliest years of her childhood in the city of Bristol, in the house on Wilson Street next door to Papa's refinery. Then, when the refinery was accidentally burned to the ground, as happened often in the sugar business, the family moved to a rambling house on Nelson Street. There, Papa's new refinery stood just across a walled-in courtyard. Each day, after their lessons, the children would go for at least one long walk. The Blackwells believed that knowledge of the natural world and vigorous physical exercise (as vigorous as the constricting clothing of the day would allow) were a crucial part of their children's education, a belief that must have struck their more conventional neighbors as just another piece of Blackwell craziness, especially in relation to the girls. It was not considered proper—or healthy—for girl children of their class to move too much.

Elizabeth dreamily wrote of "the daily walks with our

governess into the lovely environs of the then small town. We became familiar with St. Vincent's Rocks and the Hot Wells, with Clifton Down and Leigh Woods, which were not built on then. The Suspension Bridge across the Avon was a thing of the future. . . . In another direction, Mother Pugsley's field, with its healing spring, leading out of Kingsdown Parade, was a favourite walk—for passing down the fine avenue of elms we stood at the great iron gates of Sir Richard Vaughan's place, to admire the peacocks, and then passed up the lane towards Redland, where violets grew on the grassy banks and natural curiosities could be collected. All these neighborhoods were delightfully free and open . . ."

Freedom and openness—and then the return home to the house next door to a factory, and a pungent factory, at that. The sticky, sickly, cloying smell of sugarcane floated on the air the Blackwells breathed, making its way past the lilac and white jessamine that Hannah had planted in the courtyard. Some days the whole house smelled of cane.

Papa's factory was only one of many to spring up in those years when the industrial revolution was getting under way, shifting huge numbers of people from the country to the city. Men and women who might have been skilled craftspeople or farmers in earlier generations now became unskilled workers in industries like sugar refining. They crowded into cities to work, or to starve. The middle class—the factory owners—grew by leaps and bounds. So did the poor.

In Bristol in the 1830s, more than six hundred paupers lived in the poorhouse. There, fifty-eight girls shared ten beds, and eighteen beds accommodated seventy boys. The "poor laws" forced thousands of destitute parents to give up their small children, selling them into work-gangs that labored for less than a living wage or for no wage at all. Children as young as six worked. Women and girls were used in the coal mines as mules, hooked to coal carts that they dragged on hands and knees through passageways too narrow for anyone else to get through. Workers were at the mercy of their employers, who were supposed to treat them well—so the theory went—because it was in the employers' own best interest to do so.

But the theory simply didn't work. When the economic boom of the early 1820s gave way to an economic depression in the late 1820s and early 1830s, England, like the rest of Europe, hovered on the brink of revolution. Repeated riots erupted in different parts of the country, and these the government could control only by calling out the army.

In late October, 1831, it was Bristol's turn.

That fall, Elizabeth and her family were still staying in the country house they had rented for the summer in Olveston, nine miles from Bristol. Most days, she and her sisters and brothers played in the garden, which was bordered by a rapid stream straddled by two tiny bridges. Crossing them, Elizabeth found herself in a fruit-filled orchard. Here was the territory of make-believe, the domain of Robinson Crusoe. She loved to pretend she was marooned on a desert island, where she must construct her own society from scratch, far away from home. In the distance, the green Welsh mountains rose, across the Severn River, along whose winding banks the children often rambled in company with the grown-ups. Nearer to hand stood the ruins of a neighboring abbey, where wolves' heads had once been taken as tribute.

In late October, 1831, from the high ground above their house in Olveston, Elizabeth could see the city of Bristol burning. She was ten years old.

Papa had gone to work at the refinery that day, as he did every day, trotting jauntily away from the country house in a yellow carriage drawn by the pony he'd named Bessie Gray, after Elizabeth, one of whose nicknames was Bessie. Her sisters Anna and Marian had gone along with him to take their twice-weekly lessons in town. When they arrived on the outskirts of Bristol, they were stopped. The city was under siege, they were told. A mob had taken over.

The girls were terrified as Papa drove them to Nelson Street. "I forget how we reached the house," wrote Anna, "but I remember the strange appearance of the streets, entirely deserted, shops and shutters shut, nobody visible. . . . The rioters were threatening to break into Bridewell, the jail, close by the Nelson St. House, and were in possession of all the adjoining streets."

Samuel managed to bundle his two trembling daughters into the house, where he told them not to move, not to show themselves, and above all not to go outside. Then he locked them in and went off to a meeting with Bristol's other leading citizens to discuss how they might best save the city. For three days, rioters controlled Bristol. They burned down the jail, releasing all its prisoners. They burned down the town hall and the bishop's palace— these were the fires Elizabeth watched, in company with her mother, from the top of a hill nine miles away.

When the mob poured through the streets to St. Mary Redcliffe, the loveliest Anglican church in the city, determined to burn that down too, Samuel stood fearlessly out front, facing mayhem. According to Blackwell family mythology, Papa single-handedly talked the rioters out of destroying the old church, which still stands today. It is not absolutely clear what really happened, nor just what role Samuel Blackwell played, but within his family he emerged from the Bristol riots a hero.

When he and his two daughters returned in safety to Olveston, Papa sat down with his wife and sisters, and they talked. The mob violence had shaken all of them. Twelve people had been killed and nearly a hundred injured in the riots, and a huge amount of property had been destroyed. Although the Blackwell sugar refinery still stood intact, Samuel saw his future business prospects dimming. He was not immune to the widespread economic depression that had helped cause the riots in the first place. His brother James, whom he had put in charge of a branch of the business in Ireland, had managed to sink it. This was made worse a few months later by the sudden economic failure of two major sugar importers, which cost Samuel seventy thousand pounds—a fabulous sum in his day.

Then the cholera epidemic that had been raging all over England spread to Bristol.

Papa Blackwell had long dreamed of the New World. To a religious rebel, a democrat, a businessman with an enormous family whose upkeep was entirely his own responsibility, America was the promised land. A friend of his had already emigrated and was writing optimistic letters. There, Samuel thought, all of his business worries would evaporate. There, his children would not be stigmatized as Dissenters; America had no established state religion from which to dissent. His sons could go to college. His sons could become doctors or lawyers. America was the land of freedom and equality, at least for middle-class white men.

And so it was that in August, 1832, the Blackwells—all of them, Aunt Bar included—set sail for New York.

Chapter Two

Manhattan lay deserted. It was October, 1832. Cholera had swept through this city too, carried ashore by successive boatloads of European immigrants. All those New Yorkers who were in a position to leave had left. They would not return until the following spring, when the epidemic was officially declared over. Storefronts had been boarded up. Windows in family houses were curtained and shuttered. New York City was a ghost town, strange and lonely.

No one witnessed the Blackwells as they left behind New York harbor, whose clustered ships and fragrant wharves reminded them of home. They marched on rubbery sea legs through the empty streets. Their footsteps echoed against the cobblestones. Papa led the way in a claret-colored coat and a curly-brimmed beaver hat, his buff greatcoat swirling from his shoulders. At his side walked Hannah, eight months pregnant, in a gray bonnet and a matching fringed cloak, carrying *Upham's Sermons* in one hand and in the other a little beaded bag that held the family jewels. Aunt Bar marched behind them, and after her came Elizabeth, Marian, and Anna, dressed identically in slate-blue cloaks and bonnets, their muslin cuffs "fair and white as a candle." Elizabeth proudly held her mother's fringed parasol and tried to avoid being stepped on by the five youngest children, clambering along with Aunt Lucy, Aunt Mary, the governess, and the nursemaid.

When they reached their hotel near Trinity Church, the family paused for a moment. They had just spent two months in the company of hundreds of other immigrants crammed into a tiny sailing vessel that was frequently becalmed, once for a period of two full weeks. Although seasick much of the time, living on salt beef, pork, and hardtack—the only source of milk on board being an unfortunate cow who died before the journey ended—the Blackwells had endured and triumphed. They had reached their new world. Now, together, they paused and offered a prayer of thanks for the past and hope for the future. Then, while the women and children unpacked and tried to get their balance back, Samuel went off in search of the local businessmen whose names he had gathered to help him launch his new career.

Within two weeks, the family had found a house on Thompson Street, just below Washington Parade Ground (now called Washington Square), on the slightly unfashionable northern border of the city. All truly chic New Yorkers lived down around the Battery, at the southernmost tip of Manhattan, where the broad and stately avenue called Bloomingdale Road began (today it is Broadway). The avenue stretched northward for two miles, lined with majestic estates.

In contrast, their Thompson Street house stood tall and skinny, in a row of similar houses. Gone was the spaciousness of Bristol. Here, rooms were stacked one on top of the other, and Elizabeth had to use stairs to get anywhere: down to the kitchen, which was in the basement, or up to the master bedroom to peek at her new brother, George Washington Blackwell, who arrived in the New World shortly after everyone else. Behind the house was a tiny backyard, and out front at the corner of the street a communal wooden water pump. Undoubtedly, the family felt cramped here, but they had so much exploring to do that they wasted no time complaining.

Although New York City had been growing by leaps and bounds since the opening of the Erie Canal in 1825, its population was only two hundred thousand in the year the Blackwells arrived. Only one-sixth of Manhattan Island was sufficiently settled to boast paved streets. Even these were coated with mud, though they had been scraped off recently as part of the citywide clean-up to discourage the spread of cholera. Grass was occasionally visible among the cobblestones, and stray pigs roamed the streets. The remaining five-sixths of the island were comprised of farms and gardens.

In the 1830s, the commercial section of the city sorted itself out into specific streets given over to the various professions. The Blackwells went to watch the bankers and brokers at work on Wall Street. They went to Water Street to see stonecutters. Fletcher Street was where the wholesale druggists made up their potions. On Front Street, the wholesale grocers set out their colorful wares, as did the silk and leather merchants in Hanover Square.

Very quickly, the three oldest children learned to navigate New York by themselves—which was unusual, since they were female: Girls were supposed to stay close to home. But the Blackwell girls walked and walked, unchaperoned, from neighborhood to neighborhood. Elizabeth in particular grew to be a champion walker—despite her cumbersome skirts—so that by the time Sam had grown up enough to be her "companion brother," as she came to call him, she and he were known to walk as much as eighteen miles a day together. Sam shared her intellectual seriousness and her physical energy. As they walked, they discussed their spiritual life, their plans to change the imperfect world they saw around them, and the books that they were reading: Dickens' *Pickwick Papers*, for example, or the Bible, which Elizabeth spent two years reading from cover to cover, then began all over again.

Elizabeth and her siblings made friends at church and in the day schools they were now attending, and for a few years the family led a gay and varied social life. They were all musical. They loved to sing and play musical instruments together, and, despite their Methodist roots, they loved to dance. They went ice-skating and sleighing. They took trips to Peal's Museum to see the Siamese twins and to Mr. Hopper's "druggist-store" to partake of the newest thrill—soda water. There were ballooning shows, Shakespeare plays, outdoor concerts in the summer, visits to the phrenologist who read the bumps on their heads (Elizabeth's bumps reflected her impressive mind, he remarked, amidst the general hilarity).

But all was not happiness and light. Two shadows had begun to steal over the Blackwell household.

The first was political. The family had not left its

social conscience behind in England, and now a great social issue pressed itself increasingly upon them: the abolition of slavery. In 1832, America was bitterly divided on this question. In half the states, slavery was legal; in the other half, it was not. That year, the New England Anti-Slavery Society was founded, and the following year the American Anti-Slavery Society. To these organizations the Blackwells were instinctively drawn. All their values, all their beliefs led them to support abolitionism.

Their pastor, Samuel Cox, was an outspoken opponent of slavery. When lynchers threatened his life because he had "stated in the pulpit that the Lord Jesus Christ belonged to a race with darker skins than our own" (as Elizabeth later wrote), the Blackwells sheltered him for ten days. They hid escaped slaves on at least two occasions. William Lloyd Garrison, the famous emancipationist and editor of *The Liberator,* was a regular visitor to their home. Samuel had gone to hear Garrison speak at an anti-slavery meeting and was so enthused by what he heard that he leapt up on stage afterward to introduce himself, and the two men became fast friends.

From the beginning of his career, Samuel had known that the source of sugar was the cane grown in the West Indies by white planters and harvested by black slaves. But England was very far away, geographically, from the actual day-to-day experience of slavery, whereas America was not. In America, Samuel could no longer turn a blind eye to the human beings trapped within the system, nor a deaf ear to his outspoken business associates. They horrified him by explaining, among other things, that it didn't pay to "breed" slaves, but that the biggest profits came from "working them out"—that is, driving them mercilessly until they died. The average slave lasted seven years, the planters told Samuel. When a used slave died, they bought a new one.

The violence surrounding the movement for emancipation was growing. In the mid-1830s, anti-abolitionist riots broke out in Boston, during which Garrison was dragged from his offices and nearly murdered. In New York, mobs attacked the homes and churches of blacks and anti-slavery activists. During these riots, Elizabeth and her family felt compelled to lock themselves inside their home for three full days. Even so, Samuel continued to speak out in favor of abolition.

He also continued to search for alternative ways to manufacture sugar. As Elizabeth reported later, he spent long, obsessive hours attempting to make sugar from beets, which could be grown in northern climates and harvested by northern labor. He installed a furnace and boiler in the cellar of the house for his experiments, but they never panned out. Papa was the only breadwinner in the enormous Blackwell household, and he knew only one trade. He was a just man, struggling without success to disengage himself from an unjust system.

His family, meanwhile, participated more and more in the abolitionist cause. His younger children put up bags of sweets and sold them, donating the profits. His sons Sam and Henry debated the anti-abolitionists at the school they attended and frequently came home with bloody noses for their trouble—just as Samuel himself came home one night with all the buttons torn off his claret coat. His daughter Anna became a delegate to the ladies' anti-slavery convention. Elizabeth, the child clos-est to him, joined the movement ardently.

At the age of fourteen, she accompanied her older sis-ters to an anti-slavery fair in New York. At fifteen, she reported in her journal that she had been present at an American Anti-Slavery Society meeting where Garrison spoke. Her heroine was Prudence Crandall, a Quaker schoolteacher who became famous when violent threats forced her to close the racially integrated school she had been running in Connecticut. Elizabeth yearned to be as active as Prudence Crandall, but how? She was soon attending meetings of the Anti-Slavery Working Society, the Ladies' Anti-Slavery Society, the New York Anti-Slavery Society, and the Abolitionist Vigilance Committee, which helped fugitive slaves escape to Canada.

In a journal entry dated May 10, 1837, she wrote: "We went to the young men's AS meeting held at the corner of Houston & Thompson streets. Mr Birney made a short appropriate & excellent speech, Mr Burleigh a long humourous & sprited address but Prof Green's was in my opinion the jewel of the whole, he spoke on the resolu-tion "That there is no truth in the atheistic [unbelieving] cry it is of no use to plead for the slave." He showed that you benefit yourself as well as the slave by interesting your sympathies in behalf of the oppressed, & that your treatment of the helpless bleeding victim before you, naked human nature stripped of every adventitious cir-cumstance was a sure touchstone of your heart. . . ."

She was only sixteen, but already she longed to do something for the suffering slave. For the first time, she was beginning to understand how much pain people were in. She wanted to make that pain disappear, to cure the human race. She hovered halfway between an unknown future and the familiar past, between the new world of adulthood that beckoned her and the old world of the family that had not quite released her. And sometimes she identified with the oppressed, not just because her family had imbued her with a thirst for social justice, but also because she felt occasionally, in some small way, that she was one of the oppressed.

Her journal of February 27, 1837, read: "Mama told me to get out some butter & sugar, instead of which, when her back was turned I went up stairs. Papa hearing of it told Mama I should not go on with music. This made me excessively indignant. . . . I do not think that I am treated at all justly for Papa agreed to let me learn if I taught [my youngest brothers] How & Wash & I have strictly fulfilled this condition also whatever I have done, any part of my education should not be interrupted. Mama will allow Anna & Henry to be as impudent & self-willed as they please with merely a slight reproof, but directly I do any thing that does not please the strongest punishments are resorted to."

In fact, it did seem harsh of Samuel to deny his daughter music lessons. But by early 1837, he was under such enormous strain that it was understandable if he overreacted at times. This was the second shadow that had stolen over the household: The Blackwells were in serious financial trouble.

Their problems had begun a year earlier in the after-math of the disastrous fire that swept New York just before Christmas 1835. For three days, the city burned out of control, from Wall Street all the way to the Battery. It was a ferocious winter. The snow stood thigh-deep outside the house in Paulus Hook (Jersey City), where the Blackwells now lived, across the Hudson River from Manhattan. A thousand additional firemen who had set out from Baltimore and Philadelphia to help their colleagues in New York were stranded by the weather in Perth Amboy. It mattered little. Water supplies were scarce, and the temperature had dropped to seventeen degrees below zero, so whatever water firefighters aimed at burning buildings froze as it fell.

Samuel worked the pumps along with hundreds of other volunteers. On the third day, dynamite charges finally brought the fire under control. Fortunately, the Blackwell sugar refinery on Congress Street had come through the conflagration unscathed. But forty blocks of the city had been destroyed. Six hundred and forty-eight houses, stores, banks, and warehouses were gone. Thousands of inhabitants were homeless, and the economy of New York City reeled.

A week after the fire, Elizabeth and her family attended chapel in town and saw the destruction firsthand. The new Merchants Exchange had been completely gutted. Blackened ruins stood where houses had once been. In the clothing district, gutters overflowed with blackened, water-soaked silks, feathers, and velvets. Smashed casks and bottles bore sad witness to the drinking and looting that had followed the fire itself.

From that day forward, fire insurance was impossible to secure. In Samuel's business, to be uninsured was to invite catastrophe. Fire always threatened sugar refiners; the refining process itself required constantly burning furnaces. One of Samuel's sugar houses in Bristol had already gone up in flames. Now, were his business in New York to burn, he would lose everything.

For the next year, every third night he traveled into Manhattan to guard the vulnerable Congress Street sugar house.

Nonetheless, one night in late September, 1836, catastrophe struck: the whole refinery went up in flames. Beginning in a small wooden shed, the fire leapt to the main refinery building, whose interior was entirely destroyed—beams, pans, engines, boilers, and pots. The brick exterior stood like a shell, in mockery. Samuel's entire investment was gone. When his business partners, the British firm of Gower, Guppy & Company, refused to rebuild, Samuel took what little capital he had and put it in another sugar house, on Washington Street.

This building he was also obliged to guard—and obliged to sell just six months later, because his finances were so shaky.

Elizabeth understood very well the seriousness of her family's situation. She wished she could earn a living herself, but she knew it was useless to think about such things, since she was female. In March, 1837, she wrote in her journal, "What [Papa's] plans for the future are we do not know."

Chapter Three

"We are become so poor, that [Papa] has put us upon an economical plan," Elizabeth wrote in early March, 1838. "We had no meat for dinner yesterday, today we had a stew composed of potatoes with a few bones which had been carefully preserved, and *one penny leek*."

A great depression was sweeping the land, and the Blackwells were among its victims. In New York City alone, in the space of one month, 250 businesses failed and prices skyrocketed. When flour reached fifteen dollars a barrel, people rioted in the streets of Manhattan. The raging mob stoned the mayor and destroyed a thousand bushels of wheat and six hundred barrels of flour.

Samuel Blackwell was a man of his time: He was in deep financial trouble. Sugar house after sugar house had failed, and he had scarcely money to keep his household running. In "these hard times . . . all is going out and none is coming in," Elizabeth's companion-brother, Sam, wrote. "Papa is at present out of business." The family had let go their last servant and now sought paying boarders. The girls took turns doing the cooking, an activity Elizabeth especially loathed. When night fell, the family had no money to light the lamps.

Then one day at the end of March, Papa announced that they were moving to Ohio. There, he told them, he could open what would be the only refinery in the West. Their troubles would be over.

In April, they auctioned off all their furniture. The only things they kept were books, china, silver, and glassware. These they shipped ahead of them, and on May 3, they left New York for Cincinnati.

The good-byes Elizabeth said were wrenching. This time, unlike the last, she was leaving behind the city and society in which she had outgrown her childhood. She was seventeen. This time, she was leaving friends behind, and the closest of family: Aunt Bar, Aunt Lucy, Uncle Charles, and, worse, her two older sisters. Neither Anna nor Marian could afford to give up the job that she had found. Anna was earning three hundred dollars a year in Vermont, teaching music at a girls' school; Marian was teaching arithmetic in Manhattan. Elizabeth would be the oldest child in the household when she and her family set out on their daunting journey.

Just crossing the Hudson River between New Jersey and New York was dangerous. Frequently in winter, the river froze and the ferry was unable to cross or to land on the opposite side, so the Blackwell children going to school in Manhattan had sometimes had to leap from ice cake to ice cake to get ashore. Some nights they hadn't been able to get back home to Paulus Hook at all. They were always hearing accounts of shipwrecks on the Hudson or on the East River or along the Atlantic coast.

Winters were particularly chancy, but in any season traveling was dangerous and desperately uncomfortable.

And time-consuming. The Blackwells would travel more than nine continuous days to get from New York to Cincinnati.

On May 3, they went by boat from New York to Philadelphia, where they spent the night. The next day, they embarked by "rail car" for Columbia, Pennsylvania, seventy miles away. En route, they passed huge Conestoga wagons carrying freight west, and lone mailmen on dusty horseback, and occasionally a family with all its possessions heaped in a covered wagon on the way out to unsettled territories. At Columbia, they boarded a canal boat which took them along the Pennsylvania Main Line Canal as far as Pittsburgh.

In her journal, Elizabeth wrote: "4th Friday . . . We reached the canal boat & Oh what a condition we were in a room about 6 yards by 4 stuffed full of Irish women with whole trains of squalling dirty children 16 berths & the floor covered, & with the comforting assurance that we should stay till Monday morning!"

A day or so later, a broken floodgate forced passengers and cargo alike to transfer to another boat. While this was going on, Elizabeth, Sam, and Henry hiked across land to meet the rest of the family at the next lock. It was early spring, and the densely dappled forests were green with new leaves. Even back on the river, "one did not see a house for miles," Elizabeth wrote, "and the solitude was enthralling." When their boat had followed the Juniata River as far as Hollidaysburgh, the Blackwells disembarked and got aboard the Portage Railroad to cross the Allegheny Mountains.

The mountains felt like so many towering walls

thrown up between the Blackwells and the loved ones they had left behind. The mountains and the wide, wild unpredictable rivers of the New World cut the travelers off, irrevocably, from the world that they had thus far known. They felt that they might never come back again.

The Portage Railroad traveled up a series of five steep inclines, alternating with level planes—somewhat like a gigantic staircase. On level ground, passengers rode in horse-drawn carriages to the foot of each incline. There, the carriages were unhitched and attached by rope to a stationary steam engine at the top, which pulled the carriage up to the next level. Then horses took over again. In this halting and cumbersome way, the Blackwells reached the summit of the Alleghenies.

The following day, it snowed. Now they traveled by railroad to Johnstown, Pennsylvania, where they boarded another canal boat. Soon enough, they came to a break in the canal and disembarked, waiting for a steamboat to take them down the Allegheny River. The steamboat arrived, quite suddenly, at midnight, and everyone raced madly across the fog-blanketed field, scrambling for the best accommodations.

By May 10, the family had gotten as far as Pittsburgh, where an old friend from Bristol met them and took them to his home for the night, after which they still had another two days' journey ahead of them, down the Ohio River, this time in the river packet *Tribune,* to Cincinnati. The *Tribune* was steam driven—jerky, noisy, much less tranquil than the slow, hushed, horse-drawn canal boats in which the family had already spent so many hours. But the world they floated through seemed hardly modern.

River men poled flatboats and log rafts past them on the Ohio, carrying manufactured goods to the interior, and frontier products (molasses, sugar, furs, cotton, and tobacco) out to the East. The Blackwells passed log cabins on the wooded riverbanks. They watched the children of the frontier watching them steam by.

Elizabeth did not want the trip to end. She loved the traveling itself. She loved the sense of suspension between two worlds, surrounded by the stupendous natural beauty of America, continuously moving past her, continuously moving her from the known world into the vast unknown. On the twelfth of May, the family arrived in Cincinnati. Her journal for that day reads, "I was very sorry, for though pleased with the appearance of the city yet I was much grieved that the journey was over."

She was right to be grieved. Disaster lay ahead.

Distant relatives of Hannah's greeted the Blackwells at the boat and invited them home to stay, while Papa got on his feet. This he quickly did. He was an old hand at it by this time. He quickly rented a house on a hill overlooking the river. From the roof of the house, the Blackwells could see across to slave country. "The hills on the Kentucky shore opposite look very beautiful," Sam wrote to Papa's former business partner, Mr. Gower, "though in a country cursed by the demon of Opression [Sam's spelling]. . . . The land is very rich and vegetation quite rank. . . . They have a good many English customs here. Indeed I believe a third of the inhabitants and more are English, and 5/6th foreigners. . . . Everybody gets rich here somehow."

Money was on everybody's mind. Even years later,

Elizabeth would conjure up Cincinnati as "a prosperous little Western town," and indeed it had been booming since the opening of the Erie Canal, thirteen years before. Local businessmen were manufacturing boots, furniture, and stoves. Older industries, as well—tanneries, sawmills, and cotton gins—had put down roots along the banks of the Ohio, and there by the river, within a few days of his arrival, Samuel took a four-year lease on a mill. He could run his refinery for less money on water power than on steam. Only one other small refinery was operating in town. Prices here were lower than in New York, and people's spirits higher. Unlike Manhattan, the town sparkled with cleanliness. Cincinnati promised an easier life. Samuel's success was assured. Or so he thought.

Almost instantly, he discovered that the depression from which he had fled in New York City was afflicting Cincinnati too. This was no time to start a new business, even here. Certainly not for a man whose energies and self-confidence were flagging. Gamely, Samuel went out each day to talk to other businessmen, trying to drum up trade for his sugar house, trying to locate backing for his long-cherished scheme of cultivating beets.

No one was interested.

Samuel did his best to hide his sinking heart from the family. He took them for boat rides on the Ohio and picnics in the wooded hills. When their books and china and silver arrived from the East, they set up house. They chose a church to attend—Lyman Beecher's, the controversial abolitionist. They established a routine. Elizabeth gave music lessons to her younger siblings as well as to outside pupils. Henry and Sam were to begin school in the fall.

Meanwhile, they played at summer games and explored their new surroundings. "For a few months," wrote Elizabeth, "we enjoyed the strange incidents of early Western civilization, so different from the older society of the East."

The "strange incident" she chose to record in her autobiography was a Fourth of July celebration at which John Wattles, a "Come-outer," spoke. This term, Elizabeth wrote, "then applied in the West to those who were dissatisfied with every phase of social life; they were generally noticeable for their long hair and peculiar mode of dressing."

Come-outers were in fact the most active and outspoken of abolitionists. The Wattles brothers, Augustus and John, were known widely for purchasing land to give to fugitive slaves and for setting up "Humanity's Barn," a shelter for the homeless, most especially slaves in hiding. On that Independence Day of 1838, the Blackwells heard John Wattles give an anti-slavery speech, which ended with the dramatic, irrelevant cry: "Priests, Lawyers and Doctors, the Trinity of the Devil!" This was greeted by the crowd with passionate applause.

Such diversions, however, were short-lived. Quite suddenly, Papa's health began to go downhill. The summer heat in the Ohio valley was oppressive, smothering, "too much," wrote Elizabeth, "for the English constitution of our father." Samuel had suffered from malaria four years before, and now the combination of the summer weather, the stress and exhaustion of moving, and the fear of imminent financial ruin brought on a new attack. The doctors called his condition "bilious fever."

But no one really knew for certain just what bilious fever was or what to do about it—a common medical situation in 1838.

In late July, Samuel began to have fainting spells. He was prescribed the remedies of the day, calomel and sei-dlitz powders, castor oil and tartaric acid, and told to drink vitriol (sulfuric acid) in his water. This was "heroic" medicine, as it was called, at its best. The effect of all these substances was to purge the patient violently—that is, to bring on vomiting and diarrhea of such heroic propor-tions that whatever ailed him would be dynamited out of his system. The rationale underlying this practice resem-bled the rationale for the other major medical technique at that time: bleeding.

Throughout much of the nineteenth century, the sick were bled massively (with leeches and with scalpels), because it was thought that if the doctor got rid of enough blood he would relieve the "convulsive excite-ment" in the walls of his patient's blood vessels, which lay at the core of all fevers, all diseases. The famous late–eighteenth century American physician Benjamin Rush recommended removing up to four-fifths of the patient's blood. He believed, as did most of his medical colleagues for most of the nineteenth century, that "des-perate diseases require desperate remedies."

By August 1, Samuel Blackwell was desperately sick. By August 2, he was bedridden. On August 3, Elizabeth was sent to fetch his doctor at four o'clock in the morn-ing. Upon consulting with a colleague, Dr. Atlee declared that Samuel was "quite far gone." From then on, Elizabeth and Hannah stayed with him continuously, and, on August 6, Dr. Atlee himself spent the night at the patient's bedside.

Elizabeth wrote in her journal: "6th Monday . . . We all stood round his bed that night with the most intense anxiety alternately fanning him towards morning he was seized with a fit of excessive restlessness tossing from side to side rolling over & over rising up & throwing himself down again Oh twas distressing to behold, he complained of no pain but an excessive & indescribably miserable feeling afterwards his pulse began to sink alarmingly he sunk into a state of torpor, this was what the physicians dreaded."

On August 7, Samuel Blackwell died.

"He is dead . . . ," Elizabeth wrote in her journal for that day. "All agreed that salivation was the only chance left, so Mr Browne rubbed his joints with mercurial ointment several times, I spunged him with a solution of muriatic acid & through the day we gave him his medicines & as much chicken broth & brandy as he could take . . . we all knelt down around his bed, Papa's dying bed & lifted up our sorrowful hearts to him under whose stroke we were bowing. At 10 minutes past 10 he expired, . . . horrified I put my hand to his mouth & never till my dying day shall I forget the dreadful feeling when I found there was no breath it seemed so cold, then indeed we might weep without restraint & as I laid my hand on his still warm forehead what a feeling of hopeless despondency came over me."

It seemed so cold. The world seemed cold. Depopulated. Her geography had shifted. Nothing was located where it formerly had been. All former frames of reference had disappeared. Nothing would ever be the same again.

The day of the funeral, August 8, Elizabeth recorded how each member of the family cut a lock of Papa's hair, and then she kissed his cold forehead: "the features were awfully changed but still it was part of Papa."

"I felt as if all hope & joy were gone," she wrote, "& nought was left but to die also. We rode to the ground. I hated the light and the beautiful day and the people who stared at us. I seemed alone in the world."

Chapter Four

The day after Papa's funeral, Hannah and Elizabeth opened his desk and for the first time looked at his accounts. He had left them twenty dollars.

The family faced Samuel's business debts, as well as his medical and funeral expenses. The house was only half-furnished. The Blackwells had to eat. They had moved only three months earlier, and now they found themselves in a strange city, in a strange country, in desperate trouble. "We entered into the sternest realities of life," wrote Elizabeth later, "a struggle for existence without connections, without experience, with cultivated tastes, but burdened by debts which, though comparatively small, seemed formidable to us."

Elizabeth's mother was devastated by the loss of her husband and had four small children still to raise. Her youngest, Washy, was not yet six. The other adult in the house, Aunt Mary, was not nearly so strong and dynamic a second-in-command as her predecessor, Aunt Bar, who now lived a world away.

The day after the funeral, like an automaton, anesthetized by the magnitude of her loss, Elizabeth gave music lessons to her paying pupils as usual. She was at that moment the only Blackwell west of the Alleghenies who was gainfully employed. She did not know when Anna and Marian would show up in Cincinnati. They did not even know yet that their father was dead. News traveled slowly in 1838. The two oldest boys, Sam and Henry, were only fifteen and thirteen. They immediately set out to find jobs as clerks, but clearly they were not old enough to bring in much money.

It was up to Elizabeth, in conjunction with her deeply grieving mother and her unenterprising aunt, to imagine some way that they might survive. Assuming that the three of them would soon be joined by Anna and Marian, the responsibility for supporting the family would rest squarely on the shoulders of five women—in an era when women did not work. That is, ladies did not work. But one option was open to them. For a fraction of the salary men got paid, ladies were permitted to teach. Anna and Marian were already teaching in the East. If they came west and pooled their intellectual resources with Elizabeth, Aunt Mary, and Hannah, the family could open a school. Fifty private academies already existed in town. The Blackwell women could start one of their own.

Aunt Mary, Elizabeth, and Hannah did not hesitate. They put aside timidity, reluctance, and self-doubt as luxuries for which they simply did not have time. Together, they devised an advertising circular and went out into the city in search of pupils. By the end of that month, which had begun with Papa's death, Aunt Mary was instructing two boys in the front parlor while Elizabeth gave lessons to three girls in the back parlor. Her music students were increasing, and she noted in her journal on September 2, that "we had considerable additions to our pupils. Mamma had to assist me in the young ladies school."

On September 7, Anna and Marian arrived at last from the East. The faculty of the Blackwells' institution—the Cincinnati English and French Academy for Young Ladies (male pupils had already been abandoned by September)—announced that courses would now be offered in reading, writing, sketching, drawing, arithmetic, grammar, ancient and modern history, geography, natural and moral philosophy, botany, composition, French, and vocal music. All this was available for fifty dollars a year. Piano, harp, and guitar lessons were also available for an additional fifty dollars, and room and board cost two hundred dollars annually. With their meals and a place to lay their heads, all boarding students—"YOUNG LADIES residing in the Academy"—were promised "the unremitting attention of the Principal with regard to their health, comfort, improvement in personal deportment, and moral and intellectual progress."

By mid-September, the student body had grown to such an extent that large meals had to be prepared. The Blackwells hired two servants and bought a "cooking stove," which Hannah oversaw. But no sooner had the family begun to get back on its feet than Aunt Mary suddenly took sick. Incredulous, benumbed, once more incapable of doing anything to help, the Blackwell women watched as Samuel's sister died, in less than a week, of the same illness as her brother.

She had been forty-six; he had been forty-eight.

The family had scant time to mourn for her and,

worse, they had scant grief to spare, so stupefied were they still at the loss of Papa. Not two months had passed since they buried him; they could not weep for anybody else. "An awful thing is death," Elizabeth wrote. "With dear Papa our feelings were so intense that we could notice nothing but now it seemed as if whatever arrived I should never feel again not one tear did I shed, the dreadful blow we first received seems to have rendered me callous to everything else. Poor Aunt Mary she was delirious all the time took no notice of anyone, I hope I shall never die so."

Dry-eyed, the family carried on. At the academy, the number of new boarders in October forced a rearrangement of the family bedrooms. By November, matters had improved enough financially so that Elizabeth and Anna could afford to go out for the afternoon. "Mr Smith went with Anna and me to see the Giraffe," Elizabeth reported. "Tis just like the pictures of him I've seen."

Death, however, had not finished with them. Stunning news arrived from back East: Formidable Aunt Bar was gone. She and her sister Mary and her brother Samuel were all dead, suddenly, and within so short a time of one another. "How strange it seems, one after the other," wrote Elizabeth.

Elizabeth was only seventeen—or, at least, until her father's death she had been seventeen. Then, chronological age had lost all relevance. Things had changed, changed utterly, and they continued changing. She had no one to count on but herself. In early August, it had been necessary to take charge, and she had done so, stricken though she was by the loss of Papa. She was very young, but she had had to act as if she weren't. Only a year before, she had longed for some object in life and for some way of earning a living.

She was now working full time, supporting not only herself but her family. Perhaps this was the higher object she had been seeking. But it was very hard.

She missed her father terribly; she missed England. She wanted to go home. But no future seemed imaginable except more of the same, more of simply surviving the present, moment by moment. Her life consisted of twelve-hours days of intellectually barren teaching, made even worse by her fear of her students.

"I was too young and inexperienced for the undertaking," she wrote later. "I was afraid of my pupils. The elder girls were very wild Western young women, utterly unaccustomed to discipline. I only controlled them by the steady quietness of demeanor which they took for sternness, but which really was fear. They little knew how their young teacher internally quaked before her class."

This alchemy of Elizabeth's, which made her look strong, stern, and most self-confident in those moments when she was most afraid, would be crucial to her in the years ahead.

Hannah and Samuel had brought up all their children to be deeply religious, and they had also educated them—pushed them—to read and think and question and discuss. That autumn of upheaval, Elizabeth's first in Cincinnati, her first since Papa's death and the deaths of her aunts, the air was fairly shimmering with questions. Elizabeth looked to her older sister Anna for guidance and for intellectual stimulation. Anna's months in New

England had exposed her to the most advanced thinking of the day, and from the moment she arrived in Cincinnati, she and Elizabeth and Marian talked deep into the night about philosophy and religion.

The religion in which Elizabeth had been raised held no answers for her. So that fall, behind her mother's back, she and her sister Marian began to attend services at St. Paul's Cathedral, and in December they were both confirmed Episcopalian. This was a terrible blow to Mama, for Episcopalianism was America's version of the religion that had called the Blackwells second-class citizens back in England. Mama wept for the state of her daughters' souls.

She need not have worried. Within two years, the sisters had changed churches once again and, along with Anna—and the rest of the intellectual and religious vanguard of Cincinnati—had become something even worse than Episcopalians: Unitarians. "I was astonished and grieved indeed," wrote Sam, who sided with his mother, "to find how Anna and Elizabeth have imbibed the sentiments of the Unitarian church. God in His mercy protect them from it."

No such luck. The three oldest Blackwell children were now ardent followers of the new pastor of the First Congregational Church, a twenty-nine-year-old Unitarian from New England named William Henry Channing. He was a handsome young man, dark-eyed and eloquent, who preached total abstinence from liquor and immediate emancipation of the slaves. He taught that Christianity meant the universal reign of love, and he believed that human beings were innately good; he introduced his flock to transcendentalism, a new philosophy

41

which was (in Elizabeth's words) "revolutionising American thought."

Its most articulate spokesman was Ralph Waldo Emerson, a writer from Massachusetts, whose essays Elizabeth read voraciously. He confirmed her experience of the way things were. He, like she, knew the seemingly stable physical world to be unstable, unpredictable, ever-changing. Truth was not to be found in material things; it lay in human consciousness: "Mind is the only reality," he wrote.

For Emerson, all of the creation was one, unified and informed by the "oversoul," a vital force in the universe that transcended the individual. But the individual had tremendous power: "The height, the deity of man is to be self-sustained," he said, "to need no gift, no foreign force. . . . You think me the child of my circumstances: I make my circumstance. . . . You call it the power of circumstance, but it is the power of me."

I make my circumstance.

What transcendentalism offered to Elizabeth was the recognition of her own potential strength, a belief that although she could not count on the permanence of the physical world, she possessed the possibility, inherent in her self, of forging her own life.

But not immediately—the state of the Blackwell finances prevented that. Sometimes things went well; other times they did not. The year 1841 was a particularly bad year. Once again the nation's economy was in trouble. Banks and businesses were failing. The Cincinnati English and French Academy for Young Ladies was losing pupils at a dizzying rate. By March 1841, only one boarding student remained. By 1842, the school had closed.

The Blackwells' academy had failed for a number of reasons: the economic climate, a rival school that was cheaper, and the untrue rumor that all of the Blackwell women were about to get married and give up teaching. But there was also another reason for its failure.

Located just across the river from the slave-holding state of Kentucky, Cincinnati was an abolitionist center and an important stop on the Underground Railroad, which smuggled fugitive slaves out of the country to freedom. But because of its proximity to the South, the city was also a stronghold for anti-abolitionist forces. It was not unusual to see recaptured slaves being dragged back through the streets into their servitude. The escalating struggle for and against slavery was being acted out, in microcosm, in Cincinnati, and the weak economy of 1841 further divided the population. It stirred up in many whites the fear that jobs would be taken from them by freed slaves. That year anti-black riots erupted in the city. That same year William Henry Channing, who was an outspoken abolitionist, was forced by the conservatives in his parish to resign as pastor of the First Congregational Church. And the Blackwells, who were known to be friends of his, lost many of their pupils.

The failure of the academy forced the family to move to a bigger, cheaper house so that they could take in as many paying boarders as possible. This was neither the first nor the last time that such a move occurred: between the years 1838 and 1844, the family moved to five different rented houses, ever in search of more room for less money.

Everyone worked. Hannah, Marian, and the younger children ran the boardinghouse. Anna moved to Dayton to teach. Elizabeth tutored as many private pupils as she could. Sam began to look for a better-paying job. Henry dropped out of college and became a traveling salesman, peddling hardware throughout the West—teakettle lids, axes, shovels, and spittoons—and distributing anti-slavery pamphlets everywhere he went.

In 1842, the Blackwells had to be tided over by a rich relative in England, who sent them $150, and Sam remarked in his journal that the family was so low on money they were forced to jump up and down in the front parlor "in the absence of fuel to raise caloric."

But life was not all unrelenting toil and unremitting gloom. The family continued to play music, as they always had; to attend parties and go on excursions; to read widely in English, French, and German; to study (at fourteen, Emily was teaching herself Latin and gearing up to learn Greek); and to talk and talk and talk. Elizabeth spent what little spare time she had drawing, making wax flowers, and going to lectures on astronomy and women's education. She taught briefly in a black Sunday school, and, as unlikely as it seems, wrote a series of gothic mystery tales, simmering with romance.

By 1844, the family seemed relatively secure once again. Sam was working fourteen hours a day as a bookkeeper. Henry was succeeding financially in the wilderness. Anna had a teaching job back in New York and was beginning to publish articles. Then out of the blue, one day in the early spring, an offer came to the house in Cincinnati, redeemable by any one of the three oldest

Blackwell daughters: would one of them be interested in setting up a school for girls in Henderson, Kentucky?

Henderson was a small town in tobacco-growing country, way out in the western part of the state. The position paid room and board, plus four hundred dollars a year—an amount too great to refuse. But Anna was already far away, and Marian preferred to stay at home, helping her mother run the house.

Elizabeth took the job.

Chapter Five

What exactly had she gotten herself into? She had just turned twenty-three, but she had never before lived apart from her family. Now Little Shy was leaving that shelter for the wilderness, the complete unknown of Kentucky. It was heart-rending, and thrilling.

In early March 1844, Elizabeth boarded the steamboat *The Chieftain*, which carried her slowly down the Ohio River south and westward, tracing the winding watery border between Ohio and Kentucky, between the North and the South, moving ever deeper into "the crude civilization of a Western slave State" (as she wrote). After three and a half days, she was put ashore at the foot of a mud bank, her luggage in a heap beside her. *The Chieftain* had already disappeared around a bend in the river. Elizabeth gulped down her tears and gave a few convulsive laughs, then clambered up the slippery bank to have a first look at her new home.

What she saw was a dirty, straggling, country village. Her new boss, Mr. Wilson, escorted her to a small frame house. Later, in a letter to her family, she wrote, "We entered a low, shabbily furnished room, where a poorly dressed sleepy-looking woman was introduced as Mrs. Wilson." When Elizabeth indicated that she planned to start teaching in two days, her hosts reacted with deep shock: "Begin to teach on Monday! This was utterly impossible! The idea seemed to them preposterous, the schoolhouse was hardly selected, the windows were broken, the floor and walls filthy, the plaster fallen off, the responsible trustees not appointed, the scholars [her students] unnotified of my arrival."

Her heart sank.

But her obstinacy rose. Elizabeth insisted. She put her foot down. She would not budge. The sooner she began the school term, after all, the sooner it would end and the sooner she could leave.

As her adopted daughter said of her years later, Elizabeth was capable of looking "at least six feet tall" when it was necessary. That day in Henderson, she towered, all five foot one of her. She was told she could begin to teach on Monday.

She then received a tour of the small town of Henderson, and was taken to the house where she would live, in a pleasant enough room, but one she would be sharing with three other women.

The weather was miserable in March, the buildings full of chinks through which the cold came in, and the chimneys always backing up to fill the rooms with smoke. In her glacial schoolroom, she taught bundled from head to toe in her hood, her shawl, and her winter gloves. She drew her feet up onto the rung of her chair and sat like a small bird muffled against the cold.

On the first day of school, she had fourteen pupils. The number soon grew to twenty-one. And soon after that, she had to turn students away. Elizabeth was a success. Although, as she remarked to her family, people seemed to be a little afraid of her, especially when they saw her reading *Tales of Hoffman* in the original German. This was a sweet reversal for Little Shy—to be the one who was feared, instead of the one who was afraid. She had been terrorized by the "wild Western" girls who attended the Cincinnati English and French Academy for Young Ladies. Her Kentucky pupils were "much more gentle." Here, the system taught docility—at least to women and slaves—and this made her day-to-day life much easier. But it proved demoralizing after a while.

"Everyone here speaks in a whisper," Elizabeth wrote in a letter home. "I have an intense longing to scream."

She did not fit in, although she was invited to. In fact, she found she was invited far too often. People paid her too much attention. "Ever since I've been here," she wrote home, "the whole family [I live with] have treated me with kindness to the extent of their knowledge, one portion of which is never to leave me alone, and I, who so love a hermit life for a good part of the day, find myself living in public, and almost losing my identity."

Deprived of the solitude she needed, perpetually surrounded by other people, yet without any really close friends, Elizabeth felt lost. It was as though she had misplaced herself. Where *was* she?

One month after her arrival, she wrote to her family that she tried not to think of them at meals, as it upset her too much. "I used to look sentimentally to one corner of the heavens and fancy I saw you all," she wrote. Then one evening, she caught the sun setting in precisely that corner, thereby showing her that all along she had been looking in the wrong direction, west instead of east. Little Shy had lost her bearings.

She described an early and uncomfortably boring visit to some neighbors, at the end of which the whole company was asked to kneel and pray: "As we knelt down, and I looked round at the funny kneeling figures and up at the walls of a real log cabin, and on one side at the immense wood fire, it all seemed so very odd that I almost began to doubt my own identity."

She wondered who she really was, in this peculiar landscape. Nothing seemed real, not Henderson, not her self. But perhaps this was precisely what she needed. Perhaps Elizabeth had to lose her identity to find it.

She taught three days a week for ten hours straight, and gave occasional music and French lessons as well. That left a lot of vacant hours—hours and hours—unfilled. In New York and Cincinnati, in addition to her family life, there had been lectures, concerts, political meetings, a whole intellectual and cultural life. All this was entirely missing in the little town of Henderson.

The people here seemed not to speak the same language as she. They did not read the same books. They did not even have the same teeth: "I am amused to learn accidentally how I have been talked over in every direction," Elizabeth wrote, "and my teeth particularly admired. . . . 'Well, I do declare she's got a clean mouth, hasn't she!'— white teeth seeming remarkable where all use tobacco!"

Their idea of physical activity was different. Elizabeth

was a champion walker, capable of eighteen miles in Sam's company. She wrote, "The young ladies and gentlemen of Henderson are most contemptible walkers, opening wide their eyes at the idea of two or three miles, and telling doleful tales of blistered feet, wild bulls, and furious dogs, of which latter there is certainly a larger supply than at any place I have ever seen."

When summer finally came, however, the natives did walk—to a place called Lovers' Grove. In her letters home, Elizabeth described it as a lovely stretch of riverbank enclosed by trees, with hills rising behind it and a path connecting the grove to the residential section of town. She liked to walk there Sunday afternoons, until the scenery was spoiled for her by the fact that this was where the younger generation did its flirting—an activity she herself participated in, albeit briefly, escorted several times by potential suitors. As she tells it, groups of four or five young men or women would stroll out after church to meet each other "accidentally on purpose," to carve their initials in the locust trees and to watch the steamboats paddle by.

But Elizabeth had little interest in trivia and games. She quickly grew bored with Lovers' Grove and soon turned her back on it, quite literally. One day, when she'd walked out with a group of her contemporaries, she abruptly turned around and left, without a word to anyone. Later, when they asked her why she had disappeared, she laughed at them and their "sentimental doings," and they never invited her again.

Although she sometimes invented the huge family she would have in some far-distant future ("I shall present you," she wrote to her mother, "to my adorable husband, my 3 daughters, Faith, Hope, and Charity, and 4 sons, Sounding Brass, Tinkling Cymbal, Gabriel, and Beelzebub"), the fact remains that Elizabeth scorned the men she met in Henderson. "I cannot find my other half here," she wrote, "but only about a sixth, which would not do." The fact remains that she did not want to find her other half in Kentucky. For to find a husband there would have obligated her to remain, and she did not want to do that. She felt herself too different from the local population.

And her reasons were not simply frivolous.

When she wrote home to say she had "an intense longing to scream," the immediate context for this remark was a long description of slavery and her relationship to it. A letter dated April 4, 1844, reads as follows: I dislike slavery more and more every day; I suppose I see it here in its mildest form, and since my residence here I have heard of no use being made of the whipping-post, nor any instance of downright cruelty. (It was really meant as an act of hospitality when they placed a little Negro girl as a screen between me and the fire the other day!) But to live in the midst of beings degraded to the utmost in body and mind, drudging on from earliest morning to latest night, cuffed about by everyone, scolded at all day long, blamed unjustly, and without spirit enough to reply, with no consideration in any way for their feelings, with no hope for the future . . . —to live in their midst, utterly unable to help them, is to me dreadful, and what I would not do long for any consideration. Meanwhile I treat them civilly, and dispense with their services as much as possible, for which I believe the poor creatures despise me.

"The mistresses pique [vainly pride] themselves on the advantageous situation of their blacks; they positively think them very well off, and triumphantly compare their position with that of the poor in England and other countries. I endeavour, in reply, to slide in a little truth through the small apertures [openings] of their minds, for were I to come out broadly with my simple, honest opinion I should shut them up tight, arm all their prejudices, and do ten times more harm than good.

"I do long to get hold of someone to whom I can talk frankly; this constant smiling and bowing and wearing a mask provokes me intolerably . . ."

Elizabeth wanted to tear off the mask she was forced to wear, to scream at the town around her, at the politicians and the church, all of whom used Christian doctrine to justify the oppression of black people: *How can you do this?!* But Little Shy was a visitor, a guest. Cut off from her friends and family, totally alone in an alien society, she was horrified by what she saw, but she felt helpless in her isolation to do anything to effect change. For the length of her stay, it seemed, all she could do to help—or at least not to worsen—the situation was to be polite to the slaves she met, to avoid asking them to do anything, and to wait and watch for moments when she might try to shake the blind self-satisfaction of white society.

She was silent, often. Her natural shyness and her proper Victorian upbringing combined to make it virtually impossible for her to be impolite to anyone, white or black. Add to this the fact that her mother had carefully instructed her when she left home to hold her tongue or risk losing her job and the necessary money it was bringing in. Elizabeth did not want to cause offense.

After all, the people of Henderson went out of their way for her. Nor were they monsters (so she wrote). They did not whip their slaves. They were not sadists. They graciously placed a black child between their white guest and the too-hot fire, not out of cruelty to the child, but out of chivalrous consideration for Elizabeth, their visitor. They were not interested in causing the little girl pain. In fact, it probably didn't occur to them that she could feel pain. She was a slave. They moved her to shield their guest as unthinkingly as they would have moved a chair or a standing screen.

Years later in writing her autobiography, Elizabeth recalled a painful memory: "I well remember sitting with my hostess, who was reclining in her rocking-chair, on the broad, shaded verandah, one pleasant Sunday morning, listening to the distant church bells and the rustling of the locust trees, when the eldest daughter, a tall, graceful girl, dressed for Sunday, in fresh and floating summer drapery, came into the verandah on her way to church. Just at that moment a shabby, forlorn-looking negro in dirty rags approached the verandah; he was one of the slaves working in the tobacco plantation. His errand was to beg the mistress to let him have a clean shirt on that Sunday morning. The contrast of the two figures, the young lady and the slave, and the sharp reprimand with which his mistress from her rocking-chair drove the slave away, left a profound impression on my mind."

Like the sound of her own silence, her neighbors' blindness was excruciating to Elizabeth, who saw all too clearly the social injustice around her. At the end of the first term of engagement, she resigned her teaching position and returned to Cincinnati.

It was now August 1844. Elizabeth had been away for nearly half a year. She had gone to Henderson for money and experience, and she had gained these. She had demonstrated to herself that she could make it on her own, out in the great wide world. Now what? Most women of her age were married, or looking very hard to be. But Elizabeth knew that even if she were to fall in love, there was no question of devoting herself entirely to domesticity.

When she was a very little girl in Bristol, England, her grandmother Blackwell—Papa's mother, after whom Elizabeth was named—had cautioned her and her sisters against marriage. It was servitude, her grandmother had said. As Little Shy grew older, Papa had made sure to educate his daughter so well that now she found it hard to settle for what she called "ordinary" marriage. She knew too much. She wanted too much. She wanted to use her brain, her heart, her new strength, her old obstinacy to some larger purpose. She had seen terrible injustice in the South and been unable to do anything about it. She had seen suffering that she could not solace. In Henderson, she had spent her days teaching superficial lessons to nice, docile, superficial young ladies.

It was not enough.

One day, some months after her return, she was sitting at the bedside of a dying friend, Miss Donaldson. Elizabeth was talking about unimportant things, the way the healthy so often do in the presence of the very sick. The healthy so often deny what the dying know: that death is there, already, in the room.

Elizabeth spoke of her brothers Sam and Henry. They both held respectable, well-paying jobs, so that for the first time since her father's death she could afford to take a break from teaching. She remarked to her sick friend that ever since her return from Kentucky, she had been studying German, metaphysics, and music, subjects she loved; so why did they leave her unsatisfied and restless?

She described the meetings she frequently attended on abolitionism and woman's rights, the parties she and her siblings were always going to, and the literary and intellectual circles of which she was a part. All the Blackwells enjoyed writing, as had their father before them, and that year the Blackwell sisters had been invited by their friend Harriet Beecher Stowe, who would write the celebrated anti-slavery novel *Uncle Tom's Cabin* just a few years later, to join the Semi-Colon Club. At its meetings every week, Elizabeth mingled with professors, lawyers, astronomers, and authors like Stowe, who read their work aloud to the group before the evening's supper and dancing. It was an enjoyable but shapeless life.

Abruptly, her friend put out a hand to silence her.

"Elizabeth," she said, "you're fond of study. You have health and leisure. Why not study medicine?"

This was an astonishing suggestion. Women did not study medicine in 1845.

"If I could have been treated by a lady doctor," said

the friend, "my worst sufferings would have been spared me."

The sick woman was dying of cancer of the uterus, a particularly difficult disease for women of her class and generation, who had been taught to be ashamed of their anatomy and kept profoundly ignorant of how it worked. They were routinely taught to hide their physical selves from men; Victorian modesty dictated that they must. Women learned young that the very existence of the female body, especially its sexual parts, was mortifying, and that they must avoid any physical contact with the opposite sex, except as it was occasionally necessary for the making of babies.

Yet when these women got so sick that they must seek out medical attention, they were forced to go to male doctors—or to die, unattended. Many of them chose the latter course. In 1845, in America and Europe, medicine was an entirely male profession; doctors were, by definition, men. Even the traditionally female occupation of delivering babies had begun to shift from female midwives to male physicians.

But so crippling was Victorian prudery that, if a lady did happen to go to a doctor, he was not permitted to *look* while he examined her. He had to examine and treat her from behind a curtain, by feel alone; and the regular medical treatments he could offer her were often medieval. One specialist in uterine diseases, for example, urged his students to insert leeches into the womb even though, as he put it, this might "induce a paroxysm of almost intolerable suffering."

Here, then, was the predicament of Elizabeth's friend:

to be looked at by a man, to be touched by him, violated every rule she as a proper lady had been taught. And this would have been so, no matter which part of her body was ailing.

"Study medicine," Miss Donaldson said.

"I couldn't bear the sight of a medical book," Elizabeth replied, as politely as she could. The thought of becoming a doctor struck her as preposterous. "It's the study of history that appeals to me," she said, "and metaphysics." She was, after all, a transcendentalist. "I'm interested in the moral and spiritual side of life," said Elizabeth, "not the body."

"I see," came the answer.

And they dropped the subject.

But it lingered.

In her journal that night, Elizabeth noted she was "shocked by Miss Donaldson's prayer that I should become a physician." What Elizabeth was instinctively drawn to was the abstract. She did not like materialism; she was embarrassed by the body, encumbered by it. She always had been, even as a child, when she had tried repeatedly to master it. Her reaction to her friend's idea was revulsion: "The very thought of dwelling on the physical structure of the body and its various ailments filled me with disgust."

Yet the idea would not go away.

At the age of six, Elizabeth had told her older sisters that she didn't know what she would be when she grew up, but it would be something hard. Given her character—shy, squeamish, exceedingly proper, repulsed by the physical, and especially by disease—medicine would be the hardest of all the professions she might choose. Given her character—tough, obstinate, constantly self-challenging, forever testing her own limits—the fact that medicine would be hardest for her recommended it. She could not shake the idea. It haunted her.

And at this period in her life, Elizabeth's confusion about men haunted her also. She found herself struggling with the question of intimacy, of love. She had had suitors in Kentucky, but they had only clarified her sense that no flesh-and-blood creature could ever measure up to her abstract fantasy of the perfect husband. If she did not find a soul mate who could offer her emotional and intellectual companionship—and, most important, freedom to fulfill her self—she was determined not to marry.

But this was an intellectual decision. Dislike it as she might, she had a body. She had a heart, and it was, in her own words, "extremely susceptible."

An unpublished early draft of her autobiography told the following story, which she deleted from the published text: "At this very time when the medical career was suggested to me I was experiencing an unusually strong struggle between attraction towards a highly educated man with whom I had been very intimately thrown, and the distinct perception that his views were too narrow and rigid, to allow of any close and ennobling companionship.

"I grew indignant with myself, a struggle that weakened me, and resolved to take a step that I hoped might cut the knot I could not untie, and so recover full mental freedom! I finally made up my mind to devote myself to medical study, with the belief that I should thus place an insuperable barrier between myself and those disturbing influences, which I could not wisely yield to, but could not otherwise stifle. I long retained a bunch of flowers which had passed between us, done up in a packet which I sentimentally but in all sincerity labeled—young love's last dream.

"I look back now, with real pity, at the inexperience of that enthusiastic young girl, who thus hoped to stifle the master passion of human existence."

Medicine was the wall she would build against falling in love. Behind that wall, she would be safe.

Chapter Six

Sometime after the visit to her dying friend, Elizabeth began to broach the subject of medicine to those closest to her. What would you think, if . . . ?

Her first conversation was with the Stowes, liberal intellectuals who supported woman's rights. "What would you say to my becoming a doctor?" she asked them.

"Impracticable," answered Harriet Beecher Stowe. You won't get into medical school. If you do, you won't have the money to pay for it. Not to mention the time—it takes years of study. Then afterwards, how will you get patients? People would never consult a woman doctor. Forget it. It can't be done. There are too many obstacles.

Immediately, Elizabeth's interest in the project soared. I can't do it? I *shall* do it.

She began to write to physicians, asking their advice. Would it be possible . . . Do you suppose . . . ?

It would be grand, they wrote back. But it can't be done. Give it up. Whether it be Harvard or some college in the boondocks, no regular medical school in the country will admit a woman.

But this was outrageous! Simply because she was a woman, she couldn't study medicine? It was a moral injustice that her gender alone could be used against her to constrict her life, to keep her in the parlor, to deny her the power that came with knowledge and the deep pleasure of doing important work.

With each new negative response, she dug her heels in deeper: *Try to stop me.*

At that time, a growing number of "irregular" or "sectarian" medical schools allowed women to study, but these schools existed on the margins of society. They taught alternative medicine: homeopathy, for instance, whose practitioners prescribed tiny doses of remedies that produced, if given massively, the same symptoms as the disease being treated (a tiny bit of a fever-producing substance would be given to cure a fever, for instance); or hydropathy, the "water cure," based on fresh air, sunshine, exercise, and lots and lots of water taken internally and externally, in every conceivable way.

Medical sects were increasingly popular in the 1800s, especially among women who did not trust regular "heroic" medicine anymore. By 1845, "regular" doctors and scientists were seeking a more helpful, accurate understanding of sickness and health. They simply did not know very much yet. No one knew about germs or understood what caused diseases or how they spread. Not until the 1860s in America did surgeons wash their hands before they operated or disinfect their surgical instruments. In Elizabeth's time, surgeons proudly wore the same coat from operation to operation, and wiped their hands and instruments on it repeatedly. The more caked it got with old blood and who knows what else, the more respected and feared they were as surgeons. Anesthesia had not yet been discovered, and patients had to undergo surgery fully conscious. Prospective surgeons were told they needed "a strong stomach and a willingness to cut like an executioner."

Here was clearly a reason, if such were needed, for excluding the "delicate sex" from the practice of surgery: how could a lady possibly manage, emotionally or physically, to operate on a screaming, thrashing, kicking patient?

No wonder the sick turned to homeopathy or hydropathy or to some other medical sect in 1845. If sectarian doctors did not know any more than regular physicians, at least they did not torture or kill their patients with the cure itself. They did what they could to assist nature and the natural process of healing.

And they did something else that was particularly attractive to women patients: they educated them. Most sectarians believed that patients should understand their own bodies and take responsibility for their own health and hygiene; and thus sectarian doctors, many of them women, worked with woman's rights advocates to circulate educational pamphlets about the female body and to give public lectures on female physiology and anatomy. This was revolutionary, threatening to rob regular physicians—by definition, men—of their power. For the power of the physician was based, in part, on his patients' ignorance and fear.

Elizabeth respected sectarian medicine, but she was not interested in being admitted to a sectarian medical school. She refused to be marginalized in this way. She was ready to fight for the opportunity to study the most respected, scientific medicine available. She was determined to go to a mainstream medical college.

But even if she were admitted, where was she to find the money? It cost $3,000 to become a physician, an enormous sum in 1845. The Blackwell family did not have it to give. Reluctantly, Elizabeth decided she would have to teach for a while longer to scrape together some savings. When she was offered a position in Asheville, North Carolina, in a school run by the Reverend John Dickson, who had once been a doctor and could guide her initial studies in medicine, and who in addition would pay her $250 a year for every ten music students she took on, she said yes.

Elizabeth was to set off for Asheville in the middle of June. She knew it would be a difficult trip, and a difficult parting. Still, it scared her to feel, as she did deep in her bones, that she would not come home again. It scared her, too, to choose to be so different, to move away from those she loved in pursuit of a profession. Could she turn her back forever, as she felt she was doing, on the life most other women led?

It wasn't natural. As she wrote years later in her autobiography, "I felt I was severing the usual ties of life and preparing to act against my strongest natural inclinations. But a force stronger than myself then and afterwards seemed to lead me on; a purpose was before me which I must inevitably seek to accomplish."

It was of crucial importance to feel she had her family's support and belief in her. They knew that once

Elizabeth had made her mind up, the stronger her resolve would grow. They applauded her decision. Her younger sister Emily was particularly enthusiastic, and even Mama, once she had adjusted, said she only wished that Papa could have lived to see his daughter become a physician.

In mid-June, 1845, Elizabeth set out on the first leg of her journey toward her medical degree. Travel was still dangerous. The roads from Cincinnati to Asheville were so primitive that her brother Sam escorted her. Fourteen-year-old Howie went, too, so that Sam would not be alone on the long way back.

For eleven days, they jolted and jounced by horse and wagon across the rivers and mountains of Kentucky and Tennessee into North Carolina, their horse straining between the wagon shafts. The difficulty of the trip and the splendor of the scenery helped to keep Elizabeth's mind off the growing distance between her and her home. She loved "the wonderful view from the Gap of Clinch Mountain, looking down upon an ocean of mountain ridges spread out endlessly below us." And Asheville itself proved to be no Henderson, but a lovely town "en-tirely surrounded by the Alleghenies, [on] a beautiful plateau, through which the rapid French Broad River ran."

But when the time came to let go finally of the last two members of her family, Elizabeth panicked. What have I done?! she thought. What will become of me? Her brothers were going; she was on her own. In her piercing loneliness and fear, she turned to God. And what she called "the Unseen" answered her: "I retired to my bed-room and gazed from the open window long and mournfully at the dim mountain outlines visible in the starlight—mountains which seemed to shut me away hopelessly from all I cared for. Doubt and dread of what might be before me gathered in my mind. I was overwhelmed with sudden terror of what I was undertaking. In an agony of mental despair I cried out, 'Oh God, help me, support me! Lord Jesus, guide, enlighten me!' My very being went out in this yearning cry for Divine help.

"Suddenly, overwhelmingly, an answer came. A glorious presence, as of brilliant light, flooded my soul. There was nothing visible to the physical sense; but a spiritual influence so joyful, gentle, but powerful, surrounded me that the despair which had overwhelmed me vanished. All doubt as to the future, all hesitation as to the rightfulness of my purpose, left me, and never in after-life returned. I knew that, however insignificant my individual effort might be, it was in a right direction, and in accordance with the great providential ordering of our race's progress."

Elizabeth believed that the feeling flooding her at that moment came from God. She believed that her sudden certainty was "a revealed experience of Truth, a direct vision of the great reality of spiritual existence." She could lean on this belief, and did, throughout all the difficult days ahead.

In Asheville, Elizabeth could lean on her fellow human creatures too. Her hosts, the Reverend John Dickson and his wife, supported her in her project and included her in their social circle, which was more liberal and more literate than the society she had encountered in Henderson. Here (after her crisis on that first evening alone) she was much happier. She felt much more at ease, discussing transcendentalism with the Dicksons and their friends, playing the piano, demonstrating Blackwell family card tricks, and brushing off unwanted suitors. Even her hats drew praise: "My white bonnet is much admired here. Miss Charlotte Carr sent to borrow it the other day, and has made one [in] its exact image, flowers and all."

The only thing that seriously marred her stay in North Carolina was the slavery that once again surrounded her. Even the sympathetic, open-minded Reverend Dickson, who professed to believe in abolition, owned slaves. When Elizabeth asked to start a school for them, he explained that it was against the law to teach slaves how to read and write. However, he said, religious instruction was permitted, so long as it was purely oral. So Elizabeth set up a Sunday school and, raging silently at the system, explained the principles of Christianity to four little slaves, aged eight to twelve, until the authorities found out and ordered her to stop.

What cast its light over everything in Asheville, though, was that Elizabeth had found her calling. When she was not busy teaching music, French, or German, she was reading medical books loaned by the Reverend Dr. Dickson: *Oliver's First Lines of Physiology: Designed for the Use of Students of Medicine,* and *Pereira's A Treatise on Food and Diet.* Her life had taken a definite direction. Her reading now was hard and motivated.

"My brain is as busy as can be," she wrote to her mother, "and consequently I am happy."

One day, a fellow teacher laughingly placed on her

desk a large, fat, repulsive, dead beetle, which she had found smothered between two pocket handkerchiefs. Here's something to dissect, she said.

The future physician turned pale.

It may have been meant as a joke, but her colleague did not know Little Shy. As soon as Elizabeth realized her own repulsion, she couldn't not dissect the thing. She hesitated in front of it for a very long time. Every bit of her will power had to be summoned to force her to cut into the brittle shell. Her instruments were her penknife and a hairpin, and all she found inside was "a little yellowish dust." But once she had made the first incision, she was free. Never again did dissection or the study of anatomy frighten her.

By the end of July, she had performed her first "professional cure." Her patient was a Miss O'Heara, who "had just recovered from a very severe attack of illness, and great suffering in the mouth from calomel." Calomel was a mercury compound that doctors gave their patients in such huge doses that they began to water at the mouth. This was one of the first signs of acute mercury poisoning. Calomel made people throw up—and more. Their gums burned; their teeth fell out, and so did their hair; they could not speak; their tongues swelled to five times their normal size; they hallucinated, shook, ached. One of the last things done to Samuel Blackwell as he lay dying was to "salivate" him with calomel.

One day when Miss O'Heara developed a terrible headache, Elizabeth succeeded in hypnotizing it away: "I offered to relieve her, half doubting my own powers, never having attempted anything of the kind; but in a quarter or half an hour she was entirely relieved and declared some good angel had sent me to her aid."

From that day forward, Elizabeth was known as "Dr. Blackwell" in the Dickson household.

In the winter of 1846, the Reverend Dickson closed his school, which, like his own health, was failing. Elizabeth liked Asheville, but the closing of the school proved to be a stroke of luck. For John Dickson's brother, Dr. Samuel H. Dickson, happened to be an eminent physician in Charleston, South Carolina, where he served on the faculty of the medical college, and when he heard about Elizabeth and her brave career plans, he invited her to come to Charleston.

I cannot get you admitted to medical school, he said, but I will find you a job and direct your medical studies personally while you are here.

I'll come, she answered.

Elizabeth made the trip to Charleston by stagecoach and railway in January, leaving behind the wintry mountainous landscape of North Carolina for the startlingly different scenery of the Deep South. In the countryside around Charleston, the Spanish moss hung like immense webs from the trees, like the ghosts of weeping willows. The rice fields, shimmering under water, were as blue as the sky. The flat cotton fields, which stretched for hundreds of acres, belted with evergreens, were strange and beautiful. Beautiful, that is, so long as she ignored who harvested those endless acres.

Despite Charleston's beauty, the next eighteen months were drudgery, relieved only by her own study of medicine and Greek (which doctors were supposed to be able to read) and her sense of mission. She was teaching still—would she never be through with teaching?!—eight hours a day, in Madame Du Pre's boarding school. Between January, 1846, and May, 1847, Elizabeth moved doggedly forward, salting away every penny of her salary, poring over the textbooks given her by Dr. Dickson, contacting anyone she could think of for advice and assistance in becoming a physician, and trying to ignore the chorus of voices that clamored it couldn't and shouldn't be done.

The doctors with whom she now communicated expressed either vague support or outright opposition to the idea of a woman studying medicine. Sometimes, confusingly, they seemed to express both at once—as was the case with the eminent Quaker physician Dr. Joseph Warrington of Philadelphia, to whom Elizabeth wrote about her plans for the future. Dr. Warrington clearly took her very seriously; he found her sentiments extremely "noble." But his long, complicated, courteous, thoughtful, ambivalent response may be summarized as follows:

God will make thee a doctor if He wants to; it is in His hands.

However, none of *my* patients will ever consult thee (or any other woman doctor). I asked them.

Men should be physicians; women should be *nurses*.

Come see me in Philadelphia. We'll talk.

Choosing to regard this ambivalent letter as encouragement, Elizabeth sailed out of Charleston in May, 1847, bound for Philadelphia, the center of American medicine at the time. She took with her the savings she had so "carefully hoarded," as she herself put it.

It was time to storm the gates of medical school.

In Philadelphia, she boarded with Dr. William Elder, a liberal Quaker, who quickly became her friend and supporter, and immediately went to talk to Dr. Warrington. Her soft-spoken but unwavering determination quickly won him to her cause. Warrington became one of her official medical sponsors, giving her permission to attend his private medical lectures, visit his patients with him, and use his library. And he began to make inquiries for Elizabeth about her eventual admission to medical school.

Her second sponsor in Philadelphia was Dr. Jonathan M. Allen, with whom she now began to study anatomy privately. To introduce her to the intimate workings of the human body, which threatened to repulse her as a proper Victorian, Dr. Allen had the excellent taste to begin his lessons with the human wrist. She later wrote, "The beauty of the tendons and exquisite arrangements of this part of the body struck my artistic sense, and appealed to the sentiment of reverence with which this anatomical branch of study was ever afterwards invested in my mind."

Elizabeth was getting interested. New knowledge gave her a new angle of vision. She was beginning to see the world as a physician sees it. At this stage of her education, she was truly confronting her fears and finickiness, so that she would be able to plunge into medical school, excelling at it, when finally they let her. She had moved from books to anatomical models, from cadavers to living patients. She was becoming ready to become a doctor.

When she was not exploring anatomy, attending lectures, or observing Dr. Warrington with his patients, she was "interviewing" doctors affiliated with every medical school in Philadelphia. She went from one to the other, clothed as soberly and unthreateningly as she could manage, in a gray poplin dress and a little Quaker bonnet, seeking a way in.

The first words spoken by the first physician she saw, a Dr. Jackson, were: "Well? What is it? What do you want?"

I am planning to become a doctor, she said. I wish to enter medical school. Can you give me your support?

He burst out laughing.

To his credit, however, once he had listened to her, Dr. Jackson was impressed and said he would see what he could do. He soon reported, however, that all his colleagues were against admitting women. Unanimously.

Next was a Dr. Horner. The school where he taught was closed to women, he said.

As an afterthought, he suggested two other institutions she might try. They both said no.

One medical school dean rejected her not for the usual reasons—because women were too delicate, too modest, too essential to the home, and too feebleminded to be doctors—but because, on the contrary, female physicians would enjoy an unfair advantage over male physicians and steal their patients away.

Why should we give you a medical degree? he said: "You cannot expect us to furnish you with a stick to break our heads with."

Dr. Ashmead told her Paris was the only possibility, but the city was so wicked that she shouldn't even think of going there.

Dr. Pankhurst invited her to study at his college in Philadelphia—dressed as a man.

Elizabeth didn't want to go to Paris. She wanted an American medical degree. And she certainly didn't want to pose as a man. The point was to go to medical school openly, as a woman. "It was to my mind a moral crusade on which I had entered," she wrote, "a course of justice and common sense, and it must be pursued in the light of day, and with public sanction, in order to accomplish its end."

By July, all the schools in Philadelphia and New York had turned her down. Sick at heart, she began to think she would be forced to go abroad.

To put off her defeat as long as possible, she procured a list of every one of the smaller schools in the northern states, "the country schools," and picked out the twelve best and applied to them. She had by now filed twenty-nine different applications.

It was already autumn. The winter sessions at medical school were starting, and all had firmly shut their doors in her face.

Elizabeth would be twenty-seven in a matter of months. More and more, she felt the frightening rush of time and, in the pit of her stomach, a flat, heavy feeling that signaled the beginning of the death of hope.

In mid-October, as a distraction, she took a sentimental journey to New York to visit all the old familiar places with her sister Anna. She also paid a visit to her former mentor, Dr. Samuel Dickson, who had moved up recently from Charleston. She sought him out for strength, as one who had believed in her—although, of course, she wouldn't have admitted that she needed strengthening.

Finally, in early November, it was time to say good-bye to Anna and the Dicksons. With a heavy heart, Elizabeth returned to Pennsylvania.

There, on her table, amidst the usual heap of rejections, was a letter from the dean of the faculty at Geneva Medical College of Western New York (later to become Hobart College).

The dean's letter was dated October 20. It read:

"To Elizabeth Blackwell, Philadelphia.

"A quorum of the faculty assembled last evening for the first time during the session, and it was thought important to submit your proposal to the class (of students), who have had a meeting this day, and acted entirely on their own behalf, without any interference on the part of the faculty. I send you the result of their deliberations, and need only add that there are no fears but that you can, by judicious management, not only 'disarm criticism,' but elevate yourself without detracting in the least from the dignity of the profession.

"Wishing you success in your undertaking, which some may deem bold in the present state of society . . ."

Attached to this letter was the following document:

"At a meeting of the entire medical class of Geneva Medical College, held this day, October 20, 1847, the following resolutions were unanimously adopted:—

"1. Resolved—That one of the radical principles of a Republican Government is the universal education of both sexes; that to every branch of scientific education the door should be open equally to all; that the application of Elizabeth Blackwell to become a member of our class meets our entire approbation; and in extending our unanimous invitation we pledge ourselves that no conduct of ours shall cause her to regret her attendance at this institution.

"2. Resolved—That a copy of these proceedings be signed by the chairman and transmitted to Elizabeth Blackwell.

"T. J. Stratton, Chairman."

Elizabeth had been accepted. She was in—voted in by the entire student body.

She took a deep breath, glanced around to see that no one else was present, picked up her skirts, and did a wild dance for joy. Thank you! she said aloud, and laughed. Then she quickly repacked her bags. She had already missed one month of classes.

Chapter Seven

B y traveling night and day, Elizabeth reached Geneva
late on the evening of November 6. On November 7,
bright and early, she reported to the dean. She was
enrolled in Geneva Medical College as student number
130.

What she did not know until much later, and could
never have guessed from the noble language of the docu-
ments she had received, was that the faculty of the medical school was horrified at the thought of her admission.
Her application had come as a shock—and a political
problem: They did not want to admit a woman any more
than anybody else did, but they were a small rural school;
she was fully qualified to enter; and she had an influen-
tial sponsor in Dr. Joseph Warrington, whom it would
have been impolitic to offend. The faculty did not want
to be known to have turned her down for no other reason
than her gender. So they had decided to shift the responsibility for her rejection onto their students' shoulders.

The dean had gone before the student body to
announce that he had just received a letter containing
"the most extraordinary request which had ever been

made to the faculty." A lady wants to join your class, he said. Pandemonium erupted. We have decided, the dean continued, that the final decision should be yours. If you vote to admit her—unanimously—she will be admitted. One "no" vote will mean she is rejected.

It seemed obvious that someone was bound to vote against her. The professors at Geneva Medical College were saved. Or so they thought.

What they hadn't counted on was the high spirits of their students, who took the whole thing as a joke— although how the faculty could have failed to anticipate this is hard to understand: the students took all of medical school as a joke. Since there was no medical licensing at that time, virtually any male person could, with a minimum of training, call himself a doctor and get away with it; and because standards were so lax, many young men who couldn't make it as ministers or lawyers went into medicine. At Geneva Medical College, the students were mostly local boys, from small country towns, so boisterous and full of beans that the residents of the neighborhood had sent written protests a number of times, threatening to have the school closed down for disturbing the peace. During lectures, the tumult was so enormous that no one could hear the professor. And when confronted with Elizabeth's application, they went absolutely wild. They cheered, they threw things through the air, they called a meeting for that very night at which a vote was to be taken.

Every member of the class attended. Some declared they thought the application from "a lady" was a hoax, concocted by a rival medical school. Some thought it genuine—and hilarious: Just imagine a lady attending their anatomy classes! Uproarious speeches were made in support of her candidacy, and finally the vote was called.

Everybody in the room leapt up and yelled "Yea!" at the top of his lungs, except for one poor fellow, cowering in the corner.

"Nay?" he muttered.

The whole room turned around and stampeded in his direction.

He changed his vote.

This was how Elizabeth Blackwell got into medical school.

Two weeks after the riotous vote admitting a woman, her future classmates had forgotten the whole incident. One morning, as they were waiting for the first lecture of the day to begin, loafing around, telling jokes, shouting at each other across the room, and hanging out the windows of the lecture hall, making fresh remarks at the students who attended the school for girls across the way, the door at the front of the classroom opened. In walked the dean with a tragic look on his face. Clearly, something terrible had happened.

Shaking slightly, he announced that their new colleague had arrived, and with that he ushered in a young lady. She was small, shy, and simply dressed, as quiet as a Quaker. But her clear gray eyes showed sheer determination, and perhaps the slightest hint of a smile at everybody else's astonishment. She walked calmly to the front row, sat down, took off her bonnet, placed it underneath her chair, and opened her notebook.

Those who were not in their seats hurried to them,

where they remained, immobilized, for the rest of the hour. Total silence fell. When the professor started lecturing, they were able to hear what he said from start to finish for the first time all semester. The new student took notes. She was the only person in the room capable of doing so. At the end of the hour, she stood up, put her bonnet on, and exited with the professor.

And so it went, from lecture to lecture, all day long. Silence followed in her wake, and astounded, intense curiosity. It was as though a giraffe had come to medical school—except this creature wasn't a giraffe. She was a lady, and a very proper one, at that.

But a lady who was not afraid of boys. Elizabeth had played with her brothers as an equal all her life. They had been her companions. These young men who now surrounded her were just like Sam and Henry, she told herself, except they didn't know her yet. She was amused at their bewilderment, when she could get beyond her own bewilderment.

Elizabeth still possessed her old capacity to transmute inner nervousness into outward calm. None of her classmates guessed at her turmoil that first day, she looked so serene and self-assured. By the end of that first afternoon, however, her spirits had slipped. Her walk back from the school took her along the shore of white-capped Seneca Lake, lovely even under chill November skies, but all the windswept deep blue water in the world could not console her. Exhausted, she returned to her boardinghouse, where earlier the landlady (unlike the others Elizabeth approached) had sniffed that she could stay *even though she was studying medicine.*

Elizabeth felt completely at sea. She had missed four weeks of classes. She had no idea what was going on. She had no books and didn't know where to get any. She did not know her way around the school and was always going in one door and coming out another. All day long, she had been stared at, scrutinized. In the midst of scores of strangers, she was entirely alone. To make matters worse, she had heard ominous rumblings about the anatomy professor, absent that first day. He was a real character, she was told. He might quite simply bar her from his lectures. He might exclude her from the dissections that illuminated practical anatomy. These lessons were essential to her medical education.

How was she going to do this?

On the table in the dark front hall, a letter from home awaited her. She took hold of the envelope as though it were a friendly hand and, grasping it, retired to her room, which she had decorated with mementos of her far-distant siblings, her far-distant friends. The letter chattered on about the latest family news and begged for news from her. She was too gloomy to respond.

At supper, the other boarders nodded to her politely.

How do you like Geneva, Miss Blackwell? they inquired.

It is a lovely town, she said.

Have you seen the lake? they asked.

Oh yes, she said. It is a very beautiful lake.

And what brings you here? they asked.

I am a student, she said. At the medical college.

At the—?

I am studying to be a physician.

Conversation died. No one spoke to her again.

Her first night as a full-fledged medical student was long and very cold.

Chapter Eight

By morning, Elizabeth's spirits had lifted. On her second day at school, she met "a fat little fairy in the shape of the Professor of Anatomy!" who turned her world around, just as fairy godfathers were supposed to do. "Certainly I shall love fat men more than lean ones henceforth," she wrote in her journal.

Dr. Webster was warm, funny, blunt, and delighted, so he said, that Elizabeth Blackwell had joined the class. He asked what subjects she had studied, and she told him everything but surgery. At this, the dean, who was also present, paled and asked if she really meant to study that branch of medicine.

Of course she needed to know surgery, Dr. Webster replied. "Only think what a well-educated woman would do in a city like New York," he said. "Why, my dear sir, she'd have her hands full in no time; her success would be immense. Yes, yes," he told Elizabeth, "you'll go through the course, and get your diploma with great *éclat* [distinction] too; we'll give you the opportunities. You'll make a stir, I can tell you."

So I shall become a surgeon, Elizabeth thought. Yes!

That day, Dr. Webster walked ahead of her into anatomy class and read his students the letter of introduction she had brought him from Dr. Warrington. When he had finished, the class applauded. Then Elizabeth walked quietly in and took her place at the front of the room.

That night, she wrote to her mother, who was worried at her being surrounded by so many men: "I sit quietly in this large assemblage of young men, and they might be women or mummies for aught I care. I sometimes think I'm too much disciplined, but it is certainly necessary for the position I occupy. I believe the professors don't exactly know in what species of the human family to place me, and the students are a little bewildered."

Her fellow students looked at her with friendly curiosity that day, which changed soon thereafter into simple friendship. Once or twice during her first week, notes were thrown at her in class, which she ignored. "I guess my quiet manner will soon stop any nonsense," she wrote in her journal.

She was right. What began as silence and flirtatious (or malicious) mischief turned into civility, for Elizabeth was so cheerful but circumspect, so dignified and smart and clearly serious, that she won over the high-spirited young men around her. The civilizing effect of her presence—"the sudden transformation of this class from a band of lawless desperadoes to gentlemen," as one of them put it later—was to continue throughout her stay in Geneva. Many of the former desperadoes were to become her lifelong friends.

At least one fell in love with her. As she wrote to her sister Marian: "One poor fellow has certainly fallen into the depths—he waylays me at church for permission to accompany me home—he sits at college with his eyes fixed most inexpressibly upon me & starts & blushes if my eye meets his—he begged me to let him call upon me 'from the purest & most disinterested motives'" & now he is too timid to come—he is to me utterly repulsive—though a handsome fellow, I should be very sorry to let him touch my hand."

Always impatient with such devotion, Elizabeth had other things in mind. Courtship was not a part of her plan, though friendship was. She was delighted when she stopped being an oddity to her classmates and became one of them, just an ordinary medical student.

But although her academic colleagues accepted her, the town of Geneva was another matter. Elizabeth remained an object of curiosity and scandal for the duration of her stay. The townspeople, especially the women, refused to talk to her. Just like her fellow boarders on Elizabeth's long first night, they fell silent in her presence. They drew back their skirts when she walked past them in the street. They stood staring after her until she disappeared from view. They had decided that in order for a woman to attend medical school, she must be either loose and immoral, or insane. And so they stood and gaped at Little Shy, hoping to surprise her in a sudden fit of craziness or a disgusting demonstration of her secret vice.

She took to hurrying through the streets, away from them. She shut herself up in her room. She barricaded herself behind her books and her correspondence. When she could not be alone in her safe house, she sought refuge among her comrades at the college. But there the town could follow her, and did:

"You attract too much attention, Miss Blackwell," Dr. Webster laughingly said to her one day after class. "There was a very large number of strangers present this afternoon."

Quite clearly, they had not come for the sake of a medical education, but rather to sneak a look at the "doctress."

Elizabeth concentrated on the lecture and ignored them.

The dean, however, did not. Having ascertained that she was not embarrassingly unattractive, not aggressive and unladylike, but really quite presentable, he became excited about what a "good advertisement" Elizabeth might prove to the college. "I shall bring the matter into the medical journals," he said. "I'll venture to say in ten years' time one-third the classes in our colleges will consist of women. After the precedent you will have established, people's eyes will be opened."

Word that a woman had been admitted to a regular medical school did spread like wildfire in the great wide world beyond upstate New York. The *Boston Medical Journal* reported that "a pretty little specimen of the feminine gender" was studying medicine in Geneva. The *Baltimore Sun* carried the same news, adding that it hoped she would "confine her practice . . . to diseases of the heart."

In spite of these (and many more) trivializing articles in the press, Elizabeth's triumph lit up the sky of woman's rights, inspiring other women to apply to medical school—or to re-apply, if they had already tried and been rebuffed. News of Elizabeth's triumph resulted in Harvard Medical School receiving its first application from a woman. She was Harriot K. Hunt, who had been practicing homeopathy in Boston for twelve years and had established an excellent reputation, although she held no regular medical degree. When she heard about the future Dr. Blackwell, Harriot immediately applied to Harvard.

Harvard rejected her, out of hand.

Even at Geneva Medical College, in the course taught by her strongest supporter, Elizabeth soon stumbled against the same objections voiced by Harvard to a female presence in the classroom: how could any true lady "be willing in the presence of men to listen to the discussion of the subjects that necessarily [came] under the consideration of the student of medicine"? How could she so dramatically "unsex herself" and "sacrifice her modesty"? These questions arose in late November 1847, when Dr. Webster's anatomy class turned to a study of the reproductive system.

Elizabeth noted in her journal that one of the dissections immediately preceding this unit proved to be a "terrible ordeal," during which her "delicacy was certainly shocked" and all her classmates burst out laughing at their own discomfort. "I had to pinch my hand till the blood nearly came, and call on Christ to help me from smiling, for that would have ruined everything," she wrote, "but I sat in grave indifference, though the effort made my heart palpitate most painfully."

The next day, Dr. Webster wrote her a note. He was having second thoughts. His lectures on reproduction were famous for their profanity. In fact, he was notorious for his dirty jokes in all situations, but had managed to restrain himself thus far in Elizabeth's presence. In relation to the reproductive system, however, he doubted it could be done. And so he wrote to her, suggesting that she not come to class for this unit, but rather study it separately. Feminine modesty and his own masculine need to protect her from embarrassment demanded nothing else, he said.

Elizabeth's attitudes were strictly Victorian. She did not challenge the notion of feminine delicacy. What she challenged was the notion that this justified refusing a lady the exact same medical education as a gentleman. Ever since arriving in Geneva, she had been waging warfare against her own extreme modesty, especially its most visible sign—blushing. On the theory that she would not blush so easily if she could decrease the amount of blood in her body, she had been fasting for weeks. She was determined to overcome what she saw as her own weakness. She was equally determined to overcome the prejudice of others. In this newest crisis, Elizabeth set out to win the point. She wrote back to Dr. Webster.

Two days later, he arrived in class alone. Ordinarily, his female pupil accompanied him and sat in the front seat that everyone had gotten used to saving for her. Today, however, the professor announced that, since he would be lecturing on reproduction, he had asked Miss Blackwell not to be present. He read his students the note he had written to her, explaining his reasoning.

After which, he read them the letter she had written to him in reply.

She understood perfectly, she wrote, how his position might seem embarrassing, "when viewed from the low standpoint of impure and unchaste sentiments." (That is, an individual with a dirty mind might be embarrassed by the reproductive system.) However, she continued, she was sure that his mind as a medical man had been so elevated and purified by the study of the science of anatomy that such sentiments would not for a moment influence him. She herself was a serious student with a serious purpose. Anatomy was a most serious subject, exciting "profound reverence." She felt it would be a mistake for her not to come to class. If her presence in the front row made him uncomfortable, she would gladly sit in the back row and take off her bonnet, so that he would not notice her. If, of course, her fellow students did not want her in the room at all, she would comply with their wishes. Please let her know the decision.

Looking up at the class, Dr. Webster said she had been right to rebuke him. Any lady who had such a noble idea of medicine, he added, deserved everyone's encouragement and support—faculty and students alike. And with that, he opened the door.

When Elizabeth walked through it, her classmates greeted her with thunderous applause. She took her usual seat in the front row, and everyone got down to work.

According to a student who was in her class that fall—Dr. Stephen Smith, who would one day become New York City's Commissioner of Health—Dr. Webster gave the most complete and thorough course of his career that year. Just as Little Shy's presence civilized her fellow students, so it civilized their teacher too.

There were no further attempts to shelter her, for her own good, from the field she had chosen to devote her life to, and her happiness in her work grew every day. She was fascinated by her studies and touched by the support of her colleagues. "Attended the demonstrator's evening lecture—very clear—how superior to books!" she noted in her journal. "Oh, this is the way to learn! The class behaves very well, and people seem all to grow kind."

That whole autumn and deep into January, she worked like the driven young woman she was. No one stopped her. She labored weekends, nights, and early mornings to catch up with all she had missed. In anatomy, the class had covered so much ground before her late arrival that she was assigned to study privately with four of the stronger students. She did this every evening after the day's classes were done; and often, long after her four colleagues had gone home, she was still there in the classroom: "I passed hour after hour at night alone in the college, tracing out the ramification of parts, until, suddenly struck by the intense stillness around, I found that it was nearly midnight, and the rest of the little town asleep."

There were still some difficult moments, as when Dr. Webster invited her to attend his examination of a female patient in his consulting rooms. "Twas a horrible exposure," Elizabeth wrote in her journal, "indecent for any poor woman to be subjected to such a torture; she seemed to feel it, poor and ignorant as she was. I felt more than ever the necessity of my mission. But I went home out of spirits, I hardly know why. I felt alone. I must work by myself all life long."

Elizabeth seemed to recognize and identify with the humiliation felt by Dr. Webster's patient at being examined by a man—which only underlined the fact of her own gender and her own solitude. Even as she realized more dramatically than ever what a mercy it would be for women to have a woman doctor, her isolation overcame her, and it seemed to her that she would have to work, all her life, alone.

She was alone that Christmas, certainly, separate from those she cared for, reading the stories and poems her beloved family had written and collected in their "Christmas Annual." This was the anthology that the Blackwells who were still at home copied out by hand each year and shipped to those who were far away. Her journal for December 25, reads: "Christmas Day.—Bright and gay with sleighs. The lake looks most beautiful, the mist rising from it in arches, the sky a brilliant blue, and the ground covered with snow. I received my Christmas Annual with great joy; and having purchased 25 cents' worth of almonds and raisins, I had quite a cosy time reading it."

Elizabeth was leading a spartan life. She was on a stringent budget. She had to go without the occasional flowers, the perfume, the pretty things she loved. There was no money. There was only medicine.

Chapter Nine

In late January, Elizabeth returned to Philadelphia. Her classes would not resume until October. What she needed during this eight-month period was to gain clinical experience. But (it came as no surprise) no hospital would have her. Since her medical school professors had neglected to write the letters of recommendation that they had promised her, Elizabeth was at loose ends once again. In this suspended state, she began to give music lessons and tried to sell some stories she had written in order to make badly needed money.

Sometime in February, she received a letter of introduction to a member of the Guardians of the Poor, a civil commission that oversaw, among other things, Blockley Hospital and Almshouse. This was a hospital and shelter for the very poorest residents of the city. Here, if nowhere else, Elizabeth might find a position.

Like the dreadful poorhouses so vividly described in the novels of Charles Dickens, the four large buildings that housed Blockley's population of two thousand were overcrowded, underheated, poorly ventilated, and understaffed. There were not enough doctors to treat the sick, even under ordinary circumstances, and now the ranks of the sick were swollen with crowds of new Irish immigrants fleeing the famine back in Ireland. They lay on pallets on the floor at Blockley, dying of typhus, or ship fever, which they had contracted in the disease-ridden vessels en route to America. The immigrants overflowed the wards and lined the hallways. There was nowhere to put them.

With luck, this was where Elizabeth might be allowed to work.

She knew she could not serve as an official resident on the medical staff, because she did not yet have her medical degree. But when she presented her letter of introduction, she was informed that she could not even "observe hospital practices" until she had gained the support, individually, of each of the three political parties that sat on the supervisory commission. She contemplated this new obstacle for a moment. Then she straightened her bonnet and set out to lobby in her own behalf. Finally, at the end of February, she received permission to reside in the women's syphilitic wing of Blockley—the most unruly wing of the hospital—where she might study the patients as much as she liked. She moved into a room there in early March.

It was an education. She saw close up, in all its stages, not only typhus but also syphilis, a terrible disease that progressed from painful sores on the body, through insanity and paralysis, to certain death. There was no known cure. Syphilis was transmitted sexually, and many of the women suffering from it in Blockley Hospital and Almshouse were servant girls, infected and then dismissed by their employers. They were desperately ill. Elizabeth was present when one young woman tried to escape through the bars of a third-floor window by climbing down some bedsheets she had knotted together. When they came untied, she fell three stories to the ground; she lived the rest of her brief life brain-damaged and broken.

"All this is horrible!" wrote Elizabeth, whose support for woman's rights was reinforced by the wrenching vision of this victimization. More and more strongly, she became convinced that women must wrest control of their bodies from men, and that every woman should be systematically educated in hygiene, health, and morality.

Her months at Blockley were fruitful but solitary. To her great joy, her brother Sam paid her a visit in the early spring, and her brother Henry in the early fall. These visits were all too brief, however, and they brought with them news that the family was again in financial trouble. Their house was up for sale, both brothers were unsettled in their careers, Emily was now teaching and hating it, and Marian was sick. What could Elizabeth do, so far away from her loved ones and so preoccupied with her own battles?

She lived very much apart from her family—very much apart from everyone—at Blockley. The head doctor, Dr. Benedict, whom she described to her mother as "the very loveliest man the Almighty ever created," had little time for her. He was too busy with his patients. "The tears come into his eyes as he bends down to soothe some dying woman," Elizabeth wrote, "and his voice is as gentle, his touch as kind to each patient as if she were his sister. Then he is as truthful, energetic, and spirited as he is kind, so, of course, we are very good friends, though we don't see much of each other."

Sometimes she chatted briefly with the matron who ran the almshouse proper from the center of a huge central room, sunk deep in her armchair, her feet propped up on a velvet footstool, barking orders, distributing clothing, yelling at "the paupers," and punishing those who resisted her authority by forcing them to take a shower. "She is a Quaker—very pious, I believe," wrote Elizabeth. "I like to talk to her occasionally, for she is shrewd and has seen much of life through dark spectacles."

But no matter how interesting the matron's caustic comments were, she did not offer much in the way of warm human companionship. Nor did the young medical residents on the staff, who were closer to Elizabeth's age and might have been her friends, but who evidently took her presence as a threat. They hated her. Each time she walked into a ward, they pointedly walked out. When they saw that she was consulting the charts at the ends of patients' beds, they stopped writing diagnoses and treatments on them, so she was forced to guess at these. In the evening while sitting in her room, she heard stealthy footsteps in the hall and scufflings at her keyhole, as patients sneaked up to her door to try to catch a glimpse of the freak—the woman doctor. Such curiosity she treated with great good humor, though, and moved her desk into the direct line of vision of the keyhole. Let them thoroughly investigate her. This too was an education.

She wrote to her mother in August:

"Do not fear for me. I go on smoothly and healthily

at Blockley; there is really nothing pestilential amongst the diseases, and I live simply, do my duty, trust in God, and mock at the devil! . . . I often send a thought to Cincinnati as I roam through the wards and imagine our contrasted employments. . . . How I wish you could pay me another visit this summer! Well, dear mother, Heaven bless you—write me sometime. Your loving physician, E."

Little Shy had grown up. Her affection for her mother leapt from the page, but her voice was no longer that of the young girl exiled in Henderson, Kentucky, who every evening had turned in the direction of the setting sun and wished she could magically transport herself back to her family. But from now on, her location in the world would be dictated by work, not family. Elizabeth had begun to sound like a physician.

Blockley proved to be a crucial interlude—an important piece of Elizabeth's medical education. She was almost sorry to leave. Nonetheless, she wrote in her journal on September 22, 1848, "My last evening at Blockley. Here I sit writing by my first fire. How glad I am, to-morrow, to-morrow, I go home to my friends!"

Her classmates and her landlady welcomed her back. The fashionable ladies of Geneva, however, were still not speaking to her, although they no longer made a point of crossing to the opposite side of the street and turning to stare as she passed by. Elizabeth had created a real place for herself among her peers, and this was a source of great happiness. "The class seem so very friendly," she wrote in her journal. "One set me a chair, another spoke so pleasantly, and I had several little friendly chats. How little they know my sensitiveness to these trifling tokens!"

Nor did she tell them. She had traveled a great distance in one year, but Little Shy remained, deep down, as reserved as ever, and as alone. She and her classmates worked together in school, but they did not socialize outside. They were cordial colleagues, not close friends. She had chosen to marry herself to medicine. At present, this was the central relationship in her life. She would take her exams in just a few months' time. The only thing that really mattered now was studying.

She did permit herself an afternoon off in November when her brother Howie came to visit. He was seventeen now and on his way to England, where he was to apprentice himself to a cousin who ran an iron foundry. Here for one afternoon was intimacy: "How good it is to see a brother! He looked very well, and we had a merry time together. I stayed away from afternoon lectures to be with him. He is a capital companion and greatly improved. I did more laughing than I've done for months. His visit did me real good, for I have been so lonely. Heaven bless the dear boy in his future!"

She could laugh with her family as with no one else, even a brother who was ten years younger than she. After he left, Elizabeth's solitude seemed greater, especially since she knew that her sister Anna would be accompanying him to Europe. Anna was returning to the Old World that had once been their home. All the other Blackwells were in Cincinnati still. Only Elizabeth seemed to have no home.

As fall gave way to winter and the snow fell so deep that it was nearly impossible to walk through it in her long, heavy skirts, Elizabeth's studies filled her days. She had much to learn, much to do. Sometimes when "bright visions of usefulness" floated around her, Elizabeth put aside her books and—alone in her room—practiced giving lectures about social and moral reform to an immense imaginary audience. She felt sometimes such sorrow for the human race. She wanted so badly to change the world.

"I called to see the pretty blind girl operated on this morning," wrote Elizabeth in January of that year: "She was all alone in the hotel, her friends far away. Poor child! she has no protector, within or without; she asked me who the student was that brought her home, when college would be out, etc.; her simple heart and idle fancy are soon caught. Such are the women I long to surround with my stronger arm. Alas! how almost hopeless does the task seem!"

This mixing together of physical and moral health, this blurring of the lines between morality and medicine was characteristic of Elizabeth throughout her life as a physician—which she became, officially, at the end of January, 1849. A panel of her professors questioned her on every subject they had covered for two years, and she passed with flying colors. "My face burned," she wrote to Marian. "My whole being was excited, but a great load was lifted from my mind."

As Elizabeth left the examination room, she nodded to her classmates, indicating that she had passed. They cheered and crowded around her with congratulations. She felt that they genuinely supported her. This is how men and women should always be with one another, she thought, as equals, comrades. "I often feel when I am with them how beautiful the relations of man and woman might be," she wrote, "under a truer development of character, in noble circumstances."

Here was one of the direct results of her being allowed to study as an equal with men: real friendship between them.

Another was that she graduated at the head of her class.

But not without a final hiccup of resistance from the college officials. Must they really give her a degree? they wondered. Must they stick their necks out that far?

Yes! said Dr. Webster, who pointed out that she had paid her tuition and passed every course with honors. He threatened to publicize their cowardice in all the medical journals if they backed down now.

The college officials graciously decided that Elizabeth should get what was due her.

January 23, 1849, the day of the graduation ceremony, dawned as warm as summer. Elizabeth's brother Henry, who was working in New York at the time, traveled up to represent the whole family and to take notes for them on every detail of "their Elib's" triumph. This was a day to be proud of being a Blackwell.

A hour before the ceremony was to begin, not one empty seat remained in the Presbyterian church where graduation was to be held. The ladies of Geneva filled every pew. Those who had shunned Elizabeth for the past two years had come to see her graduate. One of ladies described the scene inside the church as "a vast expanse of women's bonnets and curious eyes."

"I was glad of the sudden conversion thus shown,"

Elizabeth commented, "but my past experience had given me a useful and permanent lesson at the outset of life as to the very shallow nature of popularity."

Though she could not afford it, Elizabeth had bought a new outfit for the occasion, not wishing to disgrace her family, her college, or womankind. According to an eyewitness (female), Elizabeth did not wear a hat or shawl, but "a black dress—and cape—lace collar and cuffs and her *reddishly inclined* hair was very nicely braided."

Despite the fact that Dr. Webster had urged her twice to do so, she refused to march through town, as was the custom, in the academic procession of graduates and faculty. Processions were not ladylike. Instead, she arrived in church before her colleagues, on her brother's arm, and sat at the entrance to the left aisle. "Of course when we came in," Henry noted, "there was a general stir and murmur, and everybody turned to look at us." Then the procession arrived, and her friend George Field—"a very pleasant, gentlemanly fellow-graduate," wrote Henry—offered Elizabeth his arm. She walked with him and with the rest of her class to the front pews.

The formal granting of degrees began. The president of the college gave a brief speech and then summoned four graduates at a time to the platform. Remaining seated himself, he addressed them in Latin as "Doctor" *(Domine),* doffed his hat to them, and handed them their diplomas. When all the other degrees had been conferred, he called Elizabeth up, alone. And, taking off his hat, he stood to greet her.

He saluted her as *Domina* instead of *Domine,* and conferred the medical degree on her, whereupon, wrote

Henry, "our Sis, who had walked up and stood before him with much dignity, bowed and half turned to retire, but suddenly turning back replied: 'Sir, I thank you; by the help of the Most High it shall be the effort of my life to shed honour upon your diploma.'" Then she blushed scarlet and bowed to him. The president bowed in return, and the audience burst into applause.

According to Henry, "little Dr. Webster rubbed his hands, the learned curators and faculty nodded grave approbation [approval] at each other upon the platform, and our Sis, descending the steps, took her seat with her fellow-physicians in front."

Elizabeth herself scarcely noticed the audience, transported as she was "with a sense of the grandeur of a holy life, with high resolves for the future. As I came down, George Field opened the door of the front row . . . and most gladly I obeyed the friendly invitation, feeling more thoroughly at home in the midst of these true-hearted young men than anywhere else in the town."

Dr. Blackwell had earned at last her front-row seat.

Chapter Ten

Elizabeth had triumphed. Now, like any other new M.D., she needed clinical experience in all the different areas of medicine, most particularly surgery. But unlike any other new M.D., she would most likely not be allowed into any hospital in the United States. This she knew. All her advisers told her that Paris was the only place where she would find unlimited opportunities for study in any branch of medicine.

Paris was, at midcentury, a great medical center where many American M.D.s studied for a year or so before starting to practice at home. French hospitals would not be closed to Elizabeth simply because she was a woman. Her British cousin, Kenyon, was about to return to England, and he urged her to come with him. It was time to cross the sea again.

Her ship sailed out of Boston, where she visited with her old friend and mentor William Henry Channing before she waved good-bye to her adoptive country. She watched lovely Massachusetts Bay slowly vanish in the distance, then she staggered to her berth and lay there, miserable, for five days and nights. Little Shy had come a long way since her last Atlantic crossing, but she was every bit as seasick now as she'd been then.

"How I loathe the ship!" she wrote.

And then, a week later: "Thanks be to Heaven, I am on land once more, and never do I wish again to experience that hideous nightmare—a voyage across the ocean."

She landed in England on April 30. She had been a girl of eleven when she left. In this triumphant spring of 1849, Elizabeth Blackwell was a woman of twenty-eight, and everything in the Old World struck her as new. She was enchanted at the history in which the stones around her had been steeped. She loved the castles, the colorful English gardens, even the ironworks she visited, and she wrote long letters home describing it all.

In Birmingham, she got her "first introduction to the English medical world." A well-connected friend, Charles Plevins, managed to get her an invitation to Queen's Hospital, where she was greeted with polite skepticism on the part of the doctors and all-too-familiar gawking on the part of the medical students. "It was just a repetition of old scenes," she wrote. "A few minutes' curiosity, and then all went on as usual. The students presented the same mixture of faces as our American ones, wore rather better coats, and seemed to be quicker in their movements."

Invited to witness an amputation by the hospital surgeon, Dr. Parker, she commented that she found "nothing peculiar in the operation, which was skillfully performed, without chloroform." The surgeon did not like anesthesia, she noted, so he cut off his patient's leg without it. This was business as usual in England as well as in America.

Elizabeth visited hospitals in Greenwich, London, and Hampstead, where attitudes toward a woman doctor varied—as in America—from hostile to curious to approving. Repeatedly, she was asked if she should be called "doctor." She always answered yes.

Meanwhile, she was caught up in a social whirl unlike any she had ever known. The British magazine *Punch* welcomed her with a long congratulatory poem that began:

> *Young ladies all, of every clime,*
> *Especially of Britain,*
> *Who wholly occupy your time*
> *In novels or in knitting,*
> *Whose highest skill is but to play,*
> *Sing, dance, or French to clack well,*
> *Reflect on the example, pray,*
> *Of excellent Miss Blackwell!*

In London, when she was not at a hospital or a museum, she was at one party after another. She wrote: "Engagement treads upon engagement so that I've hardly a moment to think. . . . I really enjoy it. I've never had such an experience; I must have walked ten miles a day. I come home sometimes hardly able to move a foot; I wash and dress, and in an hour I'm up again and fresh for as much more—the more I have to do, the more I can. I believe I've never yet begun to call out my power of working."

Working or playing, Elizabeth was having the time of her life. She had even discovered wine. "Iced champagne is really good," she wrote home.

Clearly, she was ready for France.

She set out for Paris in May, 1849. Whereas she had been accompanied to the unknown town of London—and vastly relieved to be—by a family friend, when it came time to go to the city she had been warned was pure wickedness, in a country whose language she spoke only haltingly, whose government had just been overthrown, whose society was in a state of turmoil, she traveled alone. She had very little money and very few people to call on in Paris for help. Once again, when it came to her career, Elizabeth was fearless.

In order to improve her French, she managed to find lodgings where she could chatter nonstop with her land-lady. She launched her first inquiries of the medical establishment as to where she might begin her training, and she awaited a response.

By mid-June, she had begun to suspect that her trusted advisers back home were mistaken. France was just as resistant as the United States to the notion of a woman doctor. Paris was indeed a great medical center. She understood why so many American M.D.s came here to complete their education. She was attending brilliant lectures at the Collège de France and the Jardin des Plantes. But what she sought was hands-on surgical training, and to her shocked surprise she was met with the same hostility she had encountered in America. The French had little use for her—this lady physician. They found her strange and possibly dangerous.

Elizabeth was reluctantly concluding that, while she awaited entry into other hospitals, she would do well to study at La Maternité, the government-run maternity hospital where French midwives were trained. Several Parisian physicians had urged her to do this. But La Maternité had its drawbacks: she was twenty-eight and a licensed physician, yet she must enter as a student, on exactly the same terms as the other students. They were untutored girls from all over France—many ten years younger than Elizabeth—who had scarcely any education at all. Then too, the school was located in the old Convent of Port Royal and run as though it were a convent still—or a prison. Once they entered, students were not permitted to leave the grounds. Every minute of every day was scheduled, from dawn to dusk. They spent their time on lectures, ward work, drills, clinics, and tests. They were not permitted to read any books or newspapers that did not pertain to medicine. They lived—and bathed—as a group; they had no privacy. The food was poor. Many of the tasks assigned were strictly menial, and every three or four nights they had night duty, during which they got no sleep at all.

But La Maternité also had its advantages. It was a great hospital, world famous. There, Elizabeth might learn to be an expert obstetrician. There, she could deliver or assist at the delivery of hundreds of babies. When she was told that she could enter for a three-month period, rather than the usual year or two required, she decided to temporarily postpone becoming the first woman surgeon in the world. On June 30, she became a "Voluntary Prisoner" (as she called herself) and entered the hospital.

She got no sleep at all on her first night inside those high, dark walls. For twelve hours she delivered babies: "A large apron of coarse towelling was given me, with the injunction [command] not to lose it, or I should have to pay three francs. [The delivery room] was a large upper room, rather dimly lighted, beds all round, a fire on the hearth, cupboards full of linen in the corners, heaps of shining copper and tin utensils, several rush-bottomed chairs and wooden tables, and in the centre a large wooden stand with sides, on which the little new-comers, tightly swathed and ticketed, are ranged side by side. In the course of the night we had the pleasure of arranging eight in this way, and the next morning when Madame Charrier [the chief midwife] made her appearance the cloth was removed and the sight shown with much triumph. It was really very droll. Each little shapeless red visage peeped from under a coarse peaked cap, on the front of which was a large label with the name and sex; a black serge jacket with a white handkerchief pinned across, and a small blanket tightly folded round the rest of the body, completed the appearance of the little mummy. . . .

"There were four young French girls sitting up with me . . . and it sounded not a little droll to hear the scientific terms flowing so glibly from their laughing lips, which were busily employed in talking nonsense all the time that their duties did not call them to the bedside."

The French girls—Elizabeth's fellow students—quickly warmed to her. "I am continually saluted with some oddly pronounced English word, followed by a burst of merriment," Elizabeth noted. The girls came to her for explanations of things they did not understand—the circulatory system, for example. They were intensely interested when she first told them she came from New York, which they seemed to think was an island near Havana. But they could hardly get over their disappointment that she was not black, as they had thought everybody in America was.

They themselves came from departments—or counties—all over France and enjoyed the kind of regional rivalry that Americans from different states enjoyed. Whenever a student gave a particularly stupid answer in class, Madame Charrier would launch a furious verbal attack, then switch to sarcasm, then to high drama— standing up abruptly, clapping her hands together, appealing to the heavens in frustration, and finally asking with exaggerated patience, in a subdued voice, "Mademoiselle, what department do you come from?"

The miserable student would answer.

"Ah," Madame Charrier would say. "Then it is all accounted for. The case is a hopeless one."

This delighted the rest of the class, who came from "more enlightened" parts of the country.

Second-year students were delegated to teach first-year students many of the basics and, because it was summer, they conducted their classes outdoors. "It is a very pretty method of instruction," wrote Elizabeth, "the young teacher seated on the grass, all the pupils grouped around under the thick shade of some fine tree, the atmosphere being of an elastic purity which is truly charming."

Much of their learning was based on pure memorization. Students simply parroted back whatever the instructor had just said, verbatim. Elizabeth already knew the substance of the lessons, the anatomy or physiology, but she did not know it in French, and memorizing terms and repeating them was the best possible way for her to learn that language. Her French improved by leaps and bounds. Nor were classes the only site of learning for her. Day and night, she got to work with actual patients (and actual leeches, "disgusting little things"). She witnessed operations, assisted at births, attended lectures, observed cases, and wrote up treatments. Here, she found, "nature . . . in great abundance to be studied."

When the medical business of the day was finished, she amused herself by writing detailed verbal portraits of individual students who touched her particularly—they too were of interest, they too constituted nature in great abundance. Of La Normande, the girl from Normandy, Elizabeth wrote: "A fresh, healthy complexion, browned by the sun and the sea air of her beautiful home, regular features, a stout, vigorous frame that has never known a touch a sickness, she walks about with a step that feels the ground; in her white quilled cap, and handkerchief pinned over her bosom, she looks with her clear blue eyes right into your face, and has a frank, loyal manner that marks her honest, independent nature. . . . She entertains [us] with her constantly overflowing life, sometimes singing, in a deep contralto voice, her peasant hymns to the Virgin—simple pathetic melodies chanted under the lindens when the day's labours are finished—or dancing vigorously the figures, more gay than graceful, of her country, while she sings some lively air. I admire her vigorous life, I like to see her in the infirmary; she tends the sick with such an honest awkwardness, such a kind heart, and lifts them like babies in her strong arms, that I see the green fields and smell the sweet country air as I watch her."

Throughout her months in La Maternité, Elizabeth brimmed with the energy and high spirits she attributed to the girls around her. Here was Little Shy in a school for younger, much less educated women, in a hospital limited to obstetrics. Yet, even here, she was able to call up her gift for writing and her sense of humor, to capture the place and the funny, naive goodness of its inhabitants.

But La Maternité was exhausting and noisy, and especially hard for a woman who so liked her privacy. At the end of a day that began at five-thirty in the morning and did not stop until the late summer darkness fell, frequently preceded by a night of no sleep whatsoever, Elizabeth would sink gratefully into her bed in the dormitory she shared with eleven others. Then a game called "promenading the beds" would begin.

She wrote home: "Our bedsteads are of iron, and placed on rollers so movable that a slight impulsion will speed them a considerable distance. . . . the favourite freak is to place a bedstead at the end of the room and drive it with great violence down the centre. The rolling noise over the brick floor is tremendous and accompanied by a regular Babel of laughter, shouting, and jokes of every description. Some get on top of their beds, which consist of three thick mattresses, and jump up and down like mad things; others get up a wild dance in one corner of the room, which grows continually faster and noisier, and the strife of tongues is truly astonishing. . . .

"The frolic ends as suddenly as it began, when, fairly full of fun, they suddenly jump into bed, say good-night, and in five minutes all are sound asleep."

Despite Elizabeth's yearning for a room of her own, she found it hard to say no when the school's head physician urged her to re-enroll at the end of her first three months. She was gifted, Monsieur Dubois told her. A full year at La Maternité would make her into "the best obstetrician, male or female, in America!"

He had a point. She was getting invaluable training, and no other hospital would yet have her. A year felt too long to delay her surgical studies, however, and much too long to live in this austere place, in this overcrowded way. Still, there was certainly more to learn here.

There was also the presence of the attending medical resident: Dr. Hippolyte Blot . . .

One of the hospital's weekly routines was vaccinations. Each student was responsible for a specific group of babies, which she brought to the Hall of Nurses and presented, squalling, one at a time, to Dr. Blot to be vaccinated. From the very beginning, Elizabeth had been directed to sit beside him so that she could observe as he "[touched] knife after knife on the arm of the infant before him." The whole idea of vaccination against disease was new, the technique revolutionary. Sometimes she had questions for him.

At first, he found it difficult to answer her. He could not meet her eyes. She seemed to embarrass him. He blushed. He ran his hand through his hair. He looked with great intensity at the baby in front of him, although he was addressing Elizabeth.

"I think he must be very young," she wrote, "or very much in awe of me."

Hippolyte Blot was indeed a few years younger than she, but gradually he got over his shyness and, as the weeks went by, became a "pleasant comrade" with whom she could discuss medicine, as she could not possibly do with the rest of the population. He told her about the discoveries of his friend Claude Bernard, the great physiologist, who was at that time exploring the circulatory and digestive systems. Once, he brought in his microscope. She found his "microscopic lecture" fascinating.

Then as he and she were finishing the day's work one afternoon, he stopped in his tracks and told her, with a suddenly formal air, that he had a request to make of her. Abruptly, he looked awkward.

Yes? she said.

He said, Would you consider—that is, if you could find the time—I would like very much to study English.

And so their English lessons began.

"I think he must have been meditating this request for some time," she wrote in her journal. "It had hardly the air of a spontaneous thought. I like him. I hope we may come a little more closely together."

Elizabeth did not feel so imprisoned at La Maternité when she was with him.

Walking the wards or strolling in the little wood behind the hospital, they had long conversations about their parents and their siblings. They discussed the future of medicine and their own medical futures. He was working toward his exams. He told her that if he were first in his class and won the gold medal, he would receive his M.D. early. Then he would be given his choice of hospital in which to work and study next year.

Elizabeth wished him the best. But she could not help thinking about the difference between the two of them. She had graduated first in her class, and she had been offered no choice at all.

In her journal she wrote, "What chance have women, shut out from these instructions?"

Well, she would make her chance. In a determined hand, she wrote: "Work on, Elizabeth!"

It is impossible to know what direction Hippolyte's and her "beautiful friendship," as she called it, might have taken if what happened next had not happened. It is clear that he figured in her decision to stay at La Maternité for another three months of study, a decision that was to change her life forever.

Chapter Eleven

In the early morning of November 4, 1849, during her fifth month at La Maternité, Elizabeth was tending an infant who had a very serious eye infection. He was threatened with blindness. In the dimly lit infirmary, she was leaning close over him to bathe his eyes when suddenly a tiny bit of liquid from them splashed up into her own left eye. She wiped it away and continued working. She was on duty for the next twelve hours, and spent the afternoon attempting to ignore the fact that her eye had begun to feel as though it had a tiny grain of sand in it. By nighttime it was swollen. By the following morning, she could not open it. The lids were stuck together.

Frightened, she hurried to her superiors and asked permission to leave temporarily, to tend to her eye.

You are being hysterical, they said. Permission is refused. Go back to work.

Hippolyte Blot was on duty. When Elizabeth went to him with her story, he examined her and ordered her into the infirmary immediately. Her left eye was badly infected, he said, and the infection was spreading to the right. She must be treated immediately. Everything depended on early treatment.

Dr. Blot marched into the director's office and explained the urgency of the situation. Then he excused himself from all his other duties and for the next few crucial days took care of Elizabeth.

Elizabeth's eyelids were cauterized. Leeches were attached to her temples. Cold compresses were put over her eyes. Her forehead was painted with opium. She was purged, given foot baths, wrapped in mustard plasters, and fed only broth. Every two hours, night and day for three full days, Hippolyte gently removed the "false membranes" forming over her eyes. The assistant midwife, Mademoiselle Mallet, alternated with him. A guard ensured absolute silence in the infirmary. In tears, all of Elizabeth's classmates came to ask for news of her. The director of the institution granted her sister Anna, who had taken an apartment nearby, the extraordinary right to visit three times every day to administer "magnetic treatments": summoning all her powers of concentration, Anna tried to beam "vital fluid" into Elizabeth's eyes by passing her hands over them.

Everyone understood what was at stake. Elizabeth was going blind. And nobody knew what to do about it. It was all very well for Hippolyte Blot to say that everything depended on early treatment. This was the middle of the nineteenth century. There was no treatment. At least, no treatment that worked.

It is unclear exactly what kind of infection Elizabeth had. She called it "purulent ophthalmia," which simply means "eye infection." What is clear is that, if she had gotten sick today, she would probably have been treated with antibiotics in the form of eye drops. Her infection would probably have cleared up in a week. But no one knew about antibiotics in 1849, nor about diseases of the eyes. The ophthalmoscope had not even been invented.

For three days, Elizabeth received around-the-clock attention from her well-meaning caretakers, and then, as she put it, the disease had done its worst. She could tell from the way those who loved her spoke—from the tone of their voices—that she was blind in her left eye.

"Ah! how dreadful it was," she wrote, "to find the daylight gradually fading as my kind doctor bent over me, and removed with an exquisite delicacy of touch the films that had formed over the pupil! I could see him for a moment clearly, but the sight soon vanished, and the eye was left in darkness."

Elizabeth refused to believe in the darkness, however. She denied it. For the next three weeks, she lay in silence in the infirmary, both eyes bandaged, willing her body to heal itself. For three weeks, this most independent of women lay deep in the dark, unable to do anything for herself and wondering if everything she had struggled for was at an end. She banished this thought instantly. But it came back, as such thoughts do. Then instantly she re-erected her defenses.

This cannot be true. This cannot happen. I refuse.

After a while, her right eye gradually opened and began to clear. Slowly it gained strength. She could get out of bed, if she was careful, and dress herself.

In her left eye, darkness abided.

Her friendship with Hippolyte had deepened during these few weeks. Before she left La Maternité, as a token of gratitude for what he had done, or tried to do, she arranged to have a gift of two elegant lamps sent to his office—to light his way. It was an exquisite gesture, and he was deeply touched. Yet he did not feel that he could thank Elizabeth directly, for this would have overstepped the bounds of propriety and broken the rules of the institution. Members of the staff were not permitted to become friends with students.

Elizabeth wrote how, after he had received her gift, "he came to me evidently full of delight and longing to be amiable, yet too conscientious to infringe the rules of the Maternité by acknowledging the present. He admired my braid of long hair, wondered how fingers without eyes could arrange anything so beautifully regular; spoke of the Protestant religion, thought if he joined any Church it would be that; turned to go, turned back again, and was evidently hardly able to leave without thanking me. . . ."

Neither she nor he ever wavered in their sense of duty. "I shall miss him exceedingly when I leave Paris," she wrote to her sister Emily, "for there is a most affectionate sympathy between us—but—a reformer's life is not a garden of roses."

Still, did she really leave him because she needed to reform the world? And how much did she wish him to be less rule-bound?

Elizabeth left La Maternité, bandaged and veiled, three weeks after her terrible accident. She said warm, tearful good-byes to everyone, and her sister took her home to her apartment on the rue de Fleurus. Once there, back in her own life, Elizabeth burst out laughing and, as she herself put it, "laughed hysterically the whole evening."

Her strange hysterical laughter resembled weeping.

She noted in her journal: "I wrote to him—how strongly my life turns to him, and yet that terrible suffering has put a distance between us that nothing can remove."

Once she was no longer a student, there were no rules to keep them apart. But the loss of her left eye, although she did not fully accept it for almost another year, apparently so shattered her that it ended any romantic thoughts there might have been.

She stayed with Anna for the next six months, months of deep anguish. Elizabeth was sick—and a miserable patient. She would have liked to walk off her sickness, to be "up and doing." Especially now. For she had been granted permission—now!—by the highest medical authorities in Paris to visit any hospitals she wished. But she couldn't. Physically, she was too weak. She could not see well enough: her left eye was useless, and her right was still so feeble that she was incapable of reading or writing. She tried to attend lectures and clinics, but she could not concentrate. Occasionally, Hippolyte paid her a visit and read to her. Occasionally, she went for walks with Anna. It was a long cruel winter, a time of great mental suffering.

Back in America, her family was heartbroken for her. Elizabeth had been the indomitable one, the unconquerable one, the Blackwell who never gave in to sickness or adversity or impossible odds. She had been their Atlas, holding the world on her shoulders. Her semi-blindness stunned them.

Emily, who had decided a year earlier to become a

doctor herself, noted in her journal: "Ah, I fear if Elizabeth be prevented from her work I shall never be able to fill her place, but I will try. The thought of her suffering hangs over me like a constant cloud."

When he first saw her damaged handwriting, Sam wrote, "Poor Elizabeth writes for the first time with her one eye. The physicians have no hope of saving the vision of the other. Elizabeth hopes still, we all hope. She can distinguish the flame of a lamp as thro. thick mist and can discern something when the hand is passed across the eye. Her sense of the greatness of loss is unspeakable."

Elizabeth tried not to speak of it.

"Fate certainly gave me a strange and sudden blow," she wrote to her uncle Charles, an ex-military man, and his wife, "but now I am up again strong & hopeful, & eager for work, & I beg uncle to feel quite sure that a brave soldier's niece will never disgrace the colours she fights under; but will be proud of the wounds gained in a great cause, & resolve more strongly than ever to 'conquer or die.' In truth, dear friends, the accident might have been so much worse that I am more disposed to rejoice than to complain. Even in its present state the eye is not a very striking disfigurement & it will gradually become still less so & then happily I never had any beauty to boast of. As to the more serious consideration—loss of vision—I still hope to recover that in time, & meanwhile the right eye grows daily stronger. . . . I still mean to be at no very distant day the first lady surgeon in the world."

In May 1850, Elizabeth received the cheering news that her cousin Kenyon had arranged for her to be admitted for official clinical training to one of the great hospitals of London—St. Bartholomew's. She would be able to make rounds on all the female wards, to observe all male wards "excepting the Syphilitic Wards," to dissect in a room "separate from the general dissecting rooms," and to study with any lecturers willing to grant permission. If she was not yet exactly the equal of her male colleagues, this was still astonishing news. For the first time in months, she felt a surge of optimism.

Before going to London, though, she must try to regain her strength completely. Otherwise, she risked ruining her opportunity at St. Bartholomew's. Determined to try anything and everything to salvage her left eye, she set out for the hydropathic establishment of Vincenz Priessnitz, who had started the whole craze for hydropathy in Europe and America. Elizabeth wrote to her sister Emily that the trip was partially research: She could broaden her medical horizons while partaking of Priessnitz's famous water cure.

She left Paris at the beginning of June and traveled for five days across France, Germany, and Prussia. At the sanitarium in Gräfenberg, she was informed by a duchess to whom she had a formal introduction that she could not, as a proper lady, stay alone in the establishment, "for it was full of gentlemen who went about in their shirt-sleeves." Elizabeth, being Elizabeth, promptly took a room there and began her hydropathic episode.

The accommodations were dismayingly rustic. She described her bed as "a wooden crib full of straw," and the food matched the living quarters in simplicity: sour and sweet milk, sour brown bread and butter at breakfast and at tea, a simple dinner of meat, vegetable and dessert at noon. Guests could supplement this diet with wild straw-berries and white rolls sold just outside the gates.

Rustic simplicity was an integral part of the cure, and it stood in marked contrast to the fanciness of the guests whom Elizabeth encountered. Many were European nobility, dressed to the nines for their simple peasant meals. Elizabeth wrote: "When the bell rang for tea I was shown into an immense hall that might seat 500 people, gaily painted, and ornamented with chandeliers, I sat down and found myself, to my utter amazement, beside a row of ladies in grand gossamer dresses with short sleeves and waists a little lower than I thought waists were ever worn; hair dressed out with curls and flowers, bracelets (I counted five on the arm next me) and rings to match! . . . People kept coming in groups, very merry, but all talking German; the gentlemen, I presume, were in shirt sleeves, but as they were all covered with coats, I was not shocked!"

Lonely at first, Elizabeth soon made friends with a young man from America, whom she described as "near-ly blind, but one of the 'smartest' fellows I ever met; quick as a flash, full of Yankee shrewdness, he bears his terrible misfortune with real heroism, and has rendered me num-berless little services."

His example gave her courage. They took the moun-tain walks together that guests were expected to take as often as they could, and they compared notes on the main feature of their treatment: water.

"Dearly beloved people," wrote Elizabeth to her fami-ly, "this cometh to you from a very watery person in a very watery place. The sound of water is heard everywhere . . ."

At six o'clock in the morning, noon, and four o'clock in the afternoon, she was sweated in blankets, plunged into cold baths, wrapped in wet bandages, seated in sitz baths, stood under showers, and made to drink glass after glass after glass of cold water. Briefly, she felt invigorated by the fresh air and exercise she was getting.

But by the end of three days, her eye began to act up again, and she wrote in her journal, "The abreibung deadens my fingers, the sitz bath gives me the colic, the wet bandages impede digestion, & tonight I went to bed with quite a feverish attack, which gave me unpleasant dreams the whole night."

So much for hydropathy.

One other disgruntled patient, discovering Elizabeth was a physician, sent for her and asked for her medical opinion. This was Madame la Princesse Obolenska, who at the end of the visit thrust some money at her, to Elizabeth's extreme embarrassment. Technically, she had been paid her first fee. This turned Dr. Blackwell into a "professional" and her casual visit into her "first regular professional consultation."

The infection in her left eye had grown worse, however, until it was more inflamed than it had been since her first attack. And so she returned to Paris, making her long journey back alone, virtually blind, "just able to open one eye for a blink of 5 seconds." She was soul-sick with the knowledge, finally, that she would not be able to save her left eye.

Once in France, she consulted the eminent French oculist Louis-Auguste Desmarres. When he had thoroughly examined her, he said that her eye would have to be removed, lest the infection spread and she become totally blind. So huge a loss seemed impossible to bear.

"Elizabeth has suffered horribly," Anna wrote to the family: "She has lost so much time, and will probably lose a good deal more before she can go on with her studies, and buoyed up she was to the last with the idea of regaining the sight of that eye (which everyone but herself knew a year ago to be quite out of the question). The certainty of its loss has been a terrible blow to her. It is indeed one of the saddest of all the many sad things I have seen in my lifetime."

It was ironic. Elizabeth, who loved metaphysics and hated the body and its illnesses, had fought to be allowed to spend her life healing illness. This fight she had won. She had become a physician. Then her own body had fallen ill, and she could not heal herself. It was ironic, too, that such a visionary pioneer should lose her vision.

Doctors operated on her in August. When the wound healed, they substituted a glass eye for the eye that she had lost.

She had also lost a dream. Elizabeth would never be a surgeon. But now at least all ambiguity was gone. She knew exactly what she had and what she did not have, what she could do and what she could not do. Now that the infected eye was gone, she had her health back. She had a long life ahead of her. She could still be a doctor.

In October, 1850, she left Paris for London.

Chapter Twelve

At first, Elizabeth scarcely recognized the brilliant city she had loved so, just the year before. It was not brilliant now. London struck her as depressing, full of "foggy smoke" that kept her from sleeping at night and made her feel sick by day. Being "a lady alone," she had some difficulty finding rooms. But she succeeded finally and moved to Thavies Inn—which, she hastened to explain to her family, was not a hotel but a quiet courtyard that she entered by an archway built underneath one of the houses on the busy street out front. Things began to look up.

She searched out her family's former minister from Bristol, Dr. Leifchild, "whose christening of me I distinctly remember!" and sent a long account of her visit to Mama. "I recognised him at once, and should have known him anywhere—fat, rosy, and laughing, notwithstanding his gray hair. I did not detect anything of the old man in him. 'Ah,' he said, 'I know that face,' and then he made me take my bonnet off and occupy a large chair by the fire."

He and she reminisced and traded gossip. He inquired what brought her to England.

"I told him I had been doing a rather singular thing; I had been studying medicine. He looked at me to see if I were in earnest, and then burst out into such a hearty, merry laugh that I joined in with all my might . . . Of course Mrs. Leifchild wanted to know what we were laughing at. 'Why, my dear, that girl there is Doctor in Medicine!' and then I must give them the whole history."

This visit joined Elizabeth's past to her present. It completed a circle and showed her just how far she had come since she was Little Shy, banished by Aunt Bar and peering through the banisters in the house in Bristol.

The next morning, she began her studies at St. Bartholomew's. Each day at nine o'clock she set out, "a little dark figure with doctorial sack and writing-case under arm," to observe the medical practice of London's most eminent physicians and to attend the lectures on pathological anatomy of the brilliant surgeon James Paget. Her first class with him was a throwback to Geneva: he asked her to wait outside the lecture room while he announced to his sixty male students who she was. Then he ushered her ceremoniously in, and they applauded, and stared. They were just as curious about her as her former colleagues in Geneva and Paris.

She spent many hours on the wards, observing the practice of "regular" medicine, and many hours outside the hospital, exploring alternative forms of healing. For the sake of her own still-fragile health, she consulted a number of "irregular" doctors, whose emphasis fell on physical exercise, fresh air, and sunshine. Dr. Blackwell had begun to know enough to recognize "the uncertainty of the art of medicine." Indeed, she had experienced it firsthand. But this caused her to wonder how she was to practice herself: what was she to do when faced with her own patients?

To her former mentor in South Carolina, Dr. Dickson, she wrote: "I am obliged to feel very sceptical as to the wisdom of much of the practice which I see pursued every day. I try very hard to believe, I continually call up my own inexperience and the superior ability of the physicians whose actions I am watching; but my doubts will not be subdued." She wanted to learn enough conventional medicine, she told him, so that she would be able not to use it, when it seemed wiser not to. She wanted to know enough so that she could "commit heresy with intelligence . . . if my convictions impel me to do it."

Elizabeth was still a Dissenter. In this, she took after Papa, although he had dissented from established religion. Elizabeth questioned established medicine.

She questioned unorthodox medicine as well. In a letter to her sister Emily, Elizabeth wrote, "It has been a heavy, perplexing subject to me on what system I should practise, for the old one appeared to me wrong, and I have thought every heresy better; but since I have been looking into these heresies a little more closely I feel as dissatisfied with them as with the old one."

What was needed was research, she wrote, "a hospital in which I can experiment; and the very instant I feel sure of any improvement I shall adopt it in my practice, in spite of a whole legion of opponents." She urged her sister to hurry up and become a doctor, "for I have really no medical friend; all the gentlemen I meet seem separated by an invincible, invisible barrier, and the women who take up the subject partially are inferior. It will not always be so; when the novelty of the innovation is past, men and women will be valuable friends in medicine, but for a time that cannot be."

At St. Bartholomew's, as elsewhere in Elizabeth's life, she had no close friends. But at least all the doctors there treated her with respect and taught her what they knew—all, that is, except for the "Professor of Midwifery and the Diseases of Women and Children": "He wrote me a very polite note, telling me that he entirely disapproved of a lady's studying medicine . . ."

It did not surprise Elizabeth that a specialist in women's diseases should reject a woman doctor. It was his patients who were the most likely to leave him and consult her. Before the nineteenth century, women had taken care of women. Childbirth and many "female complaints" had been the exclusive province of midwives. But the development of new medical technology—forceps, for instance, to assist in difficult births—was now bringing male doctors into formerly female territory, and male doctors were loath to give up their new gains. Thus, Elizabeth was shunned by the professor of midwifery at St. Bartholomew's.

Fortunately, there were other doctors, and other activities besides medicine.

One drab, gray afternoon, Elizabeth heard a knocking at the front door of her residence, and in swept three young women who had heard about her and what she had done. Bessie Raynor Parkes, Barbara Leigh Smith, and Barbara's sister Anna announced that they were fans of hers. They wanted to welcome her to England, they said. They wanted to befriend her.

And so they did. They sent flowers and put up paintings on her walls. They invited her into their families and introduced her into British society. Through them, she met the physicist Michael Faraday and the astronomer John Herschel. Elizabeth went to dinner parties with the Duchess of Buckingham, the Duke of Argyll, the Marquis of Lansdowne, and the Speaker of the House of Commons.

This was heady stuff, but it was her women friends themselves who lit up Elizabeth's life: "A bright social sun henceforth cheered the somewhat sombre atmosphere of my hospital life—I often walked home from my friends in the West between twelve and one at night (being too poor to engage cabs), not exhausted, but invigorated for the next day's work."

Elizabeth had begun to dream of a "grand moral reform society," a "wide movement of women," and here were its charter members. They were as idealistic as she, and as nonconformist—perhaps even more so. Bessie refused to wear corsets, Elizabeth told Emily, and not only that: "she won't embroider, she reads every heretic book she can get hold of, talks of following a profession, & has been known to go to an evening party, without gloves!"

Bessie became a poet, Barbara became a painter, and both remained Elizabeth's lifelong friends. That year, they introduced her to a cousin of Barbara's named Florence Nightingale, who lived unhappily with her parents in their magnificent home at Embley. A rich, proper, intense young woman of thirty, Florence wanted only to become a nurse and reform the field of nursing, but her parents would not hear of it. Nursing, they said, was a disgusting, lower-class vocation whose members were all drunks and tramps. Hospitals were not fit places for their daughter.

Dr. Blackwell spent long hours with Florence, talking about the future of women in medicine and the future of society. Elizabeth noted: "Went down with my friend Florence to Embley Park. The laurels were in full bloom. Examined the handsome house and beautiful grounds. Saturday a perfect day. Walked much with Florence in the delicious air, amid a luxury of sights and sounds. . . . As we walked on the lawn in front of the noble drawing-room she said, 'Do you know what I always think when I look at that row of windows? I think how I should turn it into a hospital ward, and just how I should place the beds!' She said she should be perfectly happy working with me, she should want no other husband."

It was Florence who first convinced Elizabeth that healthy living conditions, not heroic drugs, should be the doctor's major tools. As Florence put it, good health was threatened by the six D's: dirt, drink, diet, dampness, draughts, and drains. Here was the cornerstone of the public health movement Elizabeth would help to found, whose motto was *Prevention is better than cure.*

"Life opens to me in London," Elizabeth wrote home, "social life particularly." In May, she attended the opening of the World's Fair, where she witnessed a splendid royal procession led by Queen Victoria on Prince Albert's arm. The Crystal Palace was aglow with light. Products from around the world were on display—among them, iron ore from her Cousin Sam's mine, in an exhibit set up by her brother Howie and her cousin Kenyon.

But all of this, though entertaining, could not obscure the fact that she was feeling a familiar impatience. It was time to launch the next stage in her medical career. Elizabeth was ready now to start her practice. The only question was where.

She desperately did not want to leave London. But America was booming. It seemed the logical choice.

In 1848, the country had won its war with Mexico. Overnight, the United States had expanded to include the territories that would become Texas, New Mexico, Arizona, California, Utah, and Nevada, as well as parts of Oklahoma, Kansas, Colorado, and Wyoming. In 1849, gold had been discovered in California, and eighty thousand people stampeded west. The Gold Rush was on.

But for all its prosperity, the country was in trouble too, torn up the middle by the slavery question. California had joined the Union as a "free-soil" state (no slaves permitted within its borders) in August, 1850, very nearly causing the South to secede. The South still proudly held its slaves and now enjoyed increased support from the federal government, in the form of a stringent new Fugitive Slave Act. The United States was moving inexorably toward the Civil War.

But in the United States, the Blackwell family awaited their Elizabeth, planning a trip east to welcome her; and Elizabeth's future medical partner, her sister Emily, was now actively seeking entrance into medical school (and actively being rejected). Elizabeth had many friends in London, but no family circle to fall back on. Worse, she had no money.

New York promised to be more quickly hospitable to a woman doctor. In the United States, since her own admission to Geneva, there had sprung up two regular medical schools for women—one in Boston, one in Philadelphia—and by this time other American women were, though still with great difficulty, being admitted to formerly all-male medical schools.

With sadness, but in triumph, Elizabeth left St. Bartholomew's. Its doctors now declared that the experiment—herself—had been a success. She wept, parting from Florence Nightingale. And Elizabeth's sister Anna wept, parting from her. On Saturday, July 26, 1851, Elizabeth sailed out of Liverpool. She wrote, "I found myself at night on board ship . . . Another most important page in life fairly closed!"

Chapter Thirteen

The sign in the window said: *Furnished Rooms to Let.* She knocked.

How do you do? she said. I am Elizabeth Blackwell, Doctor in Medicine. I am looking for a room in which to open my medical practice.

The landlady looked her up and down, as though Elizabeth had just asked for a room in which to receive paying male customers or exchange messages with the dead or perform abortions. (The code word for abortionist in the nineteenth century was female physician.)

We have no vacancies, said the landlady, and shut the door in her face.

Just as all the others had. Doors were slamming shut all over New York City. Would Elizabeth never come to the end of closed doors?

She stood on the street, remembering the proper ladies of Geneva, who had whisked aside their skirts at her approach, scandalized, and who had then clamored most graciously to congratulate her once she had succeeded. She stood quite still, remembering who she was, willing herself to persevere. Then she turned, descended the steps, and crossed the street to knock at the next door advertising rooms for rent.

I am Elizabeth Blackwell, Doctor in Medicine, she said.

Go away, came the answer, room after room, door after door, in the heavy heat of August.

September was fast approaching. Elizabeth had to have a professional address where future patients could find her. She had to have a home base from which to set out on her future house calls.

Finally, reluctantly, she rented an unfurnished floor-through of rooms, which she was offered at much too high a price. She used up half her savings to furnish a bedroom and an office. There seemed to be no other choice. She put up her shingle—Elizabeth Blackwell, M.D.—and sat down to wait.

And wait.

No patients appeared.

She wandered back and forth in her sparsely furnished quarters. Day after day, she stood at the window and looked out. She wrote letters. She read until her one good eye grew weak. Sometimes she put on her bonnet and went for a walk. Then hurried back. Perhaps someone had come for her while she was gone. If so, she would never know it. The landlady refused to take her messages. Elizabeth's sign out front was scaring away other respectable women tenants, the landlady said.

In her isolation, Dr. Blackwell needed the support of other doctors. She began to pay visits to anyone she knew in her profession. Most of the physicians she saw were polite. They wished her luck, but did nothing more.

Hospitals shunned her. She applied to work at a major New York dispensary—an outpatient clinic, dispensing medical advice and medicines to the poor—in the department for women and children. She was refused.

You'll just have to start your own dispensary, won't you? the director said.

When she asked to walk the women's wards in a charity hospital, permission was withheld. Even among the poor, Dr. Blackwell was barred from practicing medicine.

But if patients eluded her, creditors did not. Their bills arrived regularly. And, mixed in with the bills, she occasionally found a nasty, abusive, anonymous letter, accusing her of doing vile things, or sometimes inviting her to do vile things. This was her only sign of recognition as a woman doctor.

The doors of scientific study, medical school, and clinical training had already slammed shut in her face, on both sides of the ocean. She had managed somehow to pry them open and slip through. Now she found the door to practice closed.

It was enraging. It called up every bit of her tenacity. In later years, Elizabeth said that she never once regretted her profession. But as she had predicted at the age of six, what she had decided to be when she grew up was very hard indeed. She wrote to her sister Emily, "I understand now why this life has never been lived before. It is hard, with no support but a high purpose, to live against every species of social opposition."

During those early New York days—when there were malicious rumors about her, but no patients—what kept Elizabeth going were the letters of support from the friends she had left in England and from her friends and family in America. She wrote back to them voluminously.

"Her letters often make me sad," commented Emily, "not from what she says, but from a sort of unhappy atmosphere. I hope as her practice increases . . . she will grow happier—at least that she will not feel the nervous oppressive discomfort that she does now."

But the very fact of Elizabeth's discomfort indicated, perhaps, that she was on the right track. She was a crusader; and crusades are not comfortable.

Meanwhile, the second (future) woman doctor in the clan, Emily, was following in her older sister's footsteps so precisely that, to make enough money for medical school, she had taken her sister's former job in Henderson. She loathed every minute of it. She considered herself a failure as a teacher and wondered sometimes if she would be any better as a doctor. Preparatory to tackling medicine, she was teaching herself Latin, Greek, French, German, and math. But her books did not save her from the turbulent self-doubt and loneliness she was suffering.

"Why am I alone," Emily wrote in her journal, "perplexed in a labyrinth of impenetrable mysteries, fettered in restraints within and without."

Even at her loneliest, Elizabeth did not seem afflicted with the kind of cosmic homesickness and self-questioning that Emily was suffering. Emily was bigger than her diminutive sister, she was more outgoing, but she lacked Little Shy's unwavering focus, her sense of herself, her faith that she knew where she wanted to go and that she would get there.

"[Elizabeth] certainly has some of the qualities of a

really great woman," Emily wrote in her journal: "she has the power of making things succeed."

Emily was now applying to medical schools and discovering that her older sister's gift for making things succeed had made it temporarily more difficult for other women to study. The very existence of one "Miss Dr. Blackwell" was a wake-up call. The voice of backlash echoed across the land: Watch out! Ladies are becoming doctors! Stop them at all cost!

School after school rejected Emily. By mid-1852, she had decided to show up for medical study at Dartmouth, uninvited. En route, she stopped in New York to visit Elizabeth. They talked nonstop for five days about medicine and society and what it might mean if they could work together as doctors. And when they had finished talking, it seemed they might actually achieve a future partnership. Elizabeth wrote that they shared "the same hopes, the same determination. . . . She has a noble intellect, clear and strong, . . . warm affections and lofty aspirations." Emily's reaction to her older sister was more pinched. "She is not nearly as particular and fidgety as I had the idea," Emily wrote in her journal.

Emily soon left for Dartmouth, but the school turned her down. Even more distressing, Geneva Medical College rejected her. The state medical association had censored the school for awarding Elizabeth a degree. Geneva had since closed its doors to women.

Don't give up, Dr. Blackwell said to her discouraged sister.

And at last, in November, Emily was accepted as a full-time student at Rush Medical College in Chicago.

Meanwhile, Elizabeth was making progress, too. In the early snowy months of 1852, broke, unemployed, quite maddened by the inactivity of her days—What was she *doing* with her M.D.? Of what use was it? Of what use was *she?*—Elizabeth had suddenly decided she would lecture. Lectures were a favorite mid-nineteenth century activity, especially among middle-class ladies. They would be her audience. Social reform would be her subject. She would talk to mothers about how to raise their girl children to change the world.

Elizabeth sat down to write, and instantly her spirits rose. At last, she was doing something meaningful, putting to use her medical knowledge, her reformist zeal, and all those hours of lecturing to the empty bedroom of her boardinghouse up in Geneva. She rented the basement of a Sunday school, and on an afternoon in early March she launched a course of lectures that would soon be published as *The Laws of Life with Special Reference to the Physical Education of Girls*.

Women should know their own bodies, preached Elizabeth, and she taught her listeners female physiology and hygiene. The stifling inactivity of most girls' childhoods ruined them, she continued, body and soul. Girls were trained to be the vapid invalids they dutifully became as women. This need not be so. Babies should not be bundled up like mummies and immobilized. Little girls should be given simple toys with which to play actively. Older girls should be encouraged to run, dance, climb, fence, ride. Develop their bodies, Elizabeth lectured. Teach them how their bodies work, give them ownership of their physical selves, and they will flourish physically and morally. And when they become women, they will save humanity.

Her beliefs grew out of her own radical upbringing: her physically active childhood, her equality with her brothers, and her parents' belief in "perfectionism." Observing women patients at Blockley, La Maternité, and Gräfenberg reinforced her own beliefs, as did her passionate conversations with reformist women like Florence Nightingale.

But she was not radical in one respect: she believed that women were morally superior to men because their ability to give birth brought them "nearer the Divine." Many women's rights supporters downplayed motherhood. Elizabeth did not. Nor was she ever a separatist. She had no interest in rejecting men. In 1850, she wrote: "I cannot sympathise fully with an anti-man movement. I have had too much kindness, aid, and just recognition from men. . . . The great object of education has nothing to do with woman's rights, or man's rights, but with the development of the human soul and body."

Nonetheless, she went on, it would be up to *women* to lead the way on the high road to moral reform.

In her audience, as she lectured on the physical education of girls, sat other women who believed as she did, many of them Quakers, and they became her earliest patients. Quaker men had been crucial to her getting into medical school. Now it was the women of this community who began to call on her to deliver their babies and consult on their children's illnesses and their own. And after the women and children in a family had been treated by Dr. Blackwell, the men sometimes risked it. Thus,

Elizabeth's practice began at last. That summer, Emily recorded in her journal that her sister had had a phenomenally successful week, during which she had seen three patients and made twenty-five dollars.

In the months that followed, Elizabeth examined her first sore throat in private practice, and her first prolapsed uterus. She also contacted a fellow physician for her first medical consultation: she was treating an elderly lady with severe pneumonia, and sought the advice of another doctor, a "kind-hearted physician" she knew from Cincinnati, who had been present at her father's death.

"This gentleman," she wrote, "after seeing the patient, went with me into the parlour. There he began to walk about the room in some agitation, exclaiming, 'A most extraordinary case! Such a one never happened to me before; I really do not know what to do!'

"I listened in surprise and much perplexity, as it was a clear case of pneumonia and no unusual degree of danger, until at last I discovered that his perplexity related to me, not to the patient, and to the propriety of consulting with a lady physician!"

Never had he worked with a woman before. He knew what to do about pneumonia. But what was he to do about Elizabeth?! It didn't seem *proper* to treat her as he would a male colleague.

"I was both amused and relieved," she wrote: "I at once assured my old acquaintance that it need not be considered in the light of an ordinary consultation, if he were uneasy about it, but as a friendly talk. So, finally he gave me his best advice; my patient rapidly got well, and happily I never afterwards had any difficulty in obtaining a necessary consultation from members of the profession."

And so Dr. Blackwell's practice kept building.

But much too slowly.

It occurred to her that with the publication of her book, *The Laws of Life,* respect for her had begun to grow. Might she not be able to find backing now to open a dispensary for the poor?

In March, 1853, Elizabeth rented a tiny room on Tompkins Square, surrounded by the overcrowded tenements of New York, and announced that three afternoons a week she would consult with patients for free. She had the financial support of a number of Quakers, and one of her new friends, Cornelia Hussey, helped her set up her consulting room. They procured a screen, some simple drugs, and linens. Then once again Elizabeth sat down to wait.

She had chosen to open her dispensary in the Eleventh Ward because of its extreme poverty and its total lack of medical services. Here, immigrant families lived in filth and fetid air, ten people to a room. Buildings had no indoor plumbing. Pigs still ran in the streets. So did blood. The major business in the quarter was the slaughterhouse. The poor had nowhere to go if they got sick, and sickness flourished like an evil flower. It was the people of this forgotten place, especially the women, whom Elizabeth wanted to serve.

Although at first they were as wary of a woman doctor as were the rich, the inhabitants of the Eleventh Ward—who had no other choice but to try and to trust—eventually welcomed her, and by January 30, 1854, less than a year after she had begun, Elizabeth was so success-ful that she was able to incorporate the New York Dispensary for Poor Women and Children.

Its board of trustees was entirely male. Its consulting physicians were all male. The only female member of the corporation was its attending physician, Dr. Elizabeth Blackwell. Very soon, she would cease to take shelter—or to camouflage herself this way—among men. But these were still early days, tricky days. She was all alone in this venture. She *was* the New York Dispensary, and she need-ed all the help she could get.

As it grew, the dispensary would give poor women access to women doctors, and women doctors access to patients. It would provide a site for the training of nurses, Elizabeth foresaw, and they in turn would teach the sick "the necessity of cleanliness, ventilation, and judicious diet." Dr. Blackwell was beginning the practice of public health. And when she offered "a word of counsel or infor-mation . . . to the destitute widow or friendless girl who was seeking work as well as health," she was beginning the practice of social work.

In cases of "extreme destitution," she even did relief work. These cases, she wrote, "have been chiefly emi-grants, mostly Germans, without friends or money, and ignorant of the language. Several families have been visit-ed where some member was sick, and found utterly desti-tute, suffering from hunger, and though honest and industrious, disappointed in every effort to obtain work. To such families a little help with money, generally in the form of a loan till work could be procured, has proved invaluable."

Elizabeth herself asked for a loan from a family friend in 1854 to buy a house at 79 East 15th Street. She immediately rented most of it to a family that took in boarders, keeping for herself only the garret where she slept and a small room in the basement, which she set up for consultations in her private practice. Somewhere in the back of her mind, however, as she handed over most of her house to strangers, glimmered an idealistic vision of a future when all the Blackwells would live together once again in New York City.

Elizabeth had reason to dream. Her practice, private and public, was looking up at last, and in February, 1854, Emily Blackwell earned her medical degree. She left America almost immediately for two years of clinical training and study in Europe, as Elizabeth had done. But Emily promised to return.

That same year there appeared in Elizabeth's life an individual who would be crucial to her medical future. On a day in late spring, a threadbare young woman knocked on Elizabeth's door. Haltingly, she inquired for Dr. Blackwell.

I am Dr. Blackwell, said Elizabeth.

My name is Marie Zakrzewska, the young woman said in a heavy German accent.

Another impoverished German immigrant, thought Elizabeth. Another patient.

The Home for the Friendless sent me here, the young woman said.

Yes, said Elizabeth. Won't you come in?

I am a professional midwife, said the stranger.

And that changed everything.

In imperfect English and—when she discovered that Elizabeth spoke it—perfect German, Marie Zakrzewska told her story:

Zak, as everybody came to call her, had grown up in Berlin, where her mother was a midwife and had trained her daughter to assist her. When she was old enough, Zak had gone for formal training to the medical college at the University of Berlin, and there she had become the protégée of the head of midwifery. Over noisy opposition (she was a woman!), he had enlisted her to teach and named her chief midwife at the hospital where he worked. She reported directly to him. After a while, she was overseeing all of obstetrics and teaching classes that numbered two hundred students.

When her mentor died, the opposition fired her.

So she had come to America, land of freedom and opportunity, believing she could practice her profession here, perhaps in the German community of New York. But every physician she talked with said the same thing: She could not be a midwife in America. Men, they said, delivered the babies here. Nor could she possibly become a physician. Women didn't, they said. They urged her to take up nursing.

She had run out of people to consult. There seemed to be nowhere left to go. To support herself, she was embroidering caps and earning fifty cents a day. She did not want to take up nursing. Did Dr. Blackwell have any advice for her?

Years later, Zak was to call that moment the beginning of her "new life in America." She was to say she could not comprehend "how Dr. Blackwell could ever have taken so deep an interest in me. . . . Yet she did. . . . She told me of her plan of founding a hospital—the long-cherished idea of my life—and said that she had opened a little dispensary on the 1st of May, two weeks before . . . and she invited me to come and assist her. She insisted that first of all I should learn English, and she offered to give me lessons twice a week and also to make efforts to enable me to enter a college to acquire the title of 'M.D.' The cordiality with which she welcomed me as a co-worker, I can never describe or forget. . . . All the days of disappointment were instantly forgotten."

For Elizabeth too, the meeting was capital. "I have at last found a student in whom I can take a great deal of interest," she wrote to Emily. "There is true stuff in her, and I shall do my best to bring it out. She must obtain a medical degree."

Elizabeth set about teaching Zak English. She arranged to have her admitted to Western Reserve and found sponsors to pay Zak's expenses. That fall of 1854, the young German woman entered medical school in Cleveland, with the promise that she would come back to New York City to work with Dr. Blackwell in two years.

"We may reckon on a little group of three," Elizabeth wrote to Emily.

It sounded like the end of loneliness.

Chapter Fourteen

In 1854, the group of three was still a fantasy. Emily was in Scotland. Zak was in Ohio. Elizabeth lived in isolation still, as solitary as she had ever been.

One night, long after dark, as she was returning from a house call, she suddenly heard footsteps in the silent New York street behind her. She quickened her pace.

"Turn right," she heard a male voice whisper at her elbow. "Turn at the corner there."

She glanced sideways to see a well-dressed man looking her up and down appraisingly, as though she were a prostitute.

Elizabeth turned on him a glacial stare. Goodnight, she said as frigidly as she was able, and continued walking.

She heard his hastily retreating footsteps echo in the empty streets.

On other nights, she found herself hurrying past groups of drunken merrymakers who jeered, "See that lone woman walking like mad?!"

She wished she were invisible.

Even the police—the guardians of the law—made trouble for her. Several times, as she waited after dark for a horse-drawn trolley in front of City Hall, a policeman approached and tried to grab her.

She did not find such assaults frightening. The city seemed no more dangerous than the little upstate town where she had often walked home alone from medical school at midnight. But these unpleasant episodes and the insolent letters she received and the malicious gossip that she heard about herself made her feel all the more alone.

"I am woman as well as physician," she wrote to Emily, "and both natures are wounded by these falsehoods." They wore her down, and there was no one in New York to comfort her.

Elizabeth was thirty-three and had lived apart from her family for more than eight years. She continued to cherish the work she was doing. "How good work is—work that has a soul in it! I cannot conceive that anything can supply its want to a woman. In all human relations the woman has to yield, to modify her individuality—the strong personality of even the best husband and children compels some daily sacrifice of self. . . . but true work is perfect freedom, and full satisfaction."

Yes, but what about close human bonds?

"The utter loneliness of life became intolerable," she was to write, years later, about this period of her life.

One day in October, 1854, Elizabeth visited a state-run orphanage on Randall's Island. She later wrote to Emily: "I must tell you of a little item that I've introduced into my own domestic economy in the shape of a small girl between 7 and 8 years old, whom I mean to train up into a valuable domestic [servant], if she prove on sufficient trial to have the qualities, I give her credit for. I chose her out of 400 children at Randall's Island, no easy thing to do—but I have been satisfied so far of the wisdom of my choice.

"She is an orphan, no living soul claims her, her name even seems doubtful, but she is called Catharine Barry—she was a plain, and they said stupid child though good, and they all wondered at my choice—I thought otherwise, she wanted to come with me, no difficulty was made, I gave a receipt for her, and the poor little thing trotted after me like a dog.

"Instead of being stupid, I find now that she is withdrawn from blows and tyranny, that she is very bright, has able little fingers that are learning to dust, and wash up, and sew, and much perseverance and energy for so small a child—she is a sturdy little thing, affectionate and with a touch of obstinacy which will turn to good account later in life. Of course she is more trouble than use at present, and quite bewildered me at first, but still I like on the whole to have her, and it is quite pretty to hear her in the morning, sitting up in bed, waiting for permission to get up, and singing. . . . She is not pretty, but has an honest little face, something like Howard's when a young child—and it is growing brighter every day under happier influences than the poor child has ever yet known."

All Elizabeth wanted was a servant, she claimed.

But whatever her motives for bringing Kitty into her home, by the time Elizabeth turned thirty-five two years later, the child had won her. In her journal Elizabeth wrote (for no one's eyes but her own): "On this bright Sunday morning I feel full of hope and strength for the future. Kitty plays beside me with her doll. She has just given me a candy basket, purchased with a penny she had earned, full of delight in 'Doctor's birthday'! Who will ever guess the restorative support which that poor little orphan has been to me? When I took her to live with me she was about seven and a half years old. I desperately needed the change of thought she compelled me to give her. It was a dark time, and she did me good—her genial, loyal, Irish temperament suited me. Now I look forward with much hope to the coming events of this year."

The little Irish orphan had claimed her heart. Kitty offered warmth; she softened and charmed Dr. Blackwell and was entirely devoted to the woman she always called "My Doctor." To Elizabeth, who felt she was herself an orphan of sorts, Kitty's complete devotion was the greatest of gifts.

Just how thoroughly Elizabeth had formed Kitty was clear the day the child remarked in perplexity, after a male physician's visit to them, "How very odd it is to hear a *man* called 'Doctor'!"

Elizabeth was not the only Blackwell of her generation to begin a family at this time. Within a period of two years, Henry and Sam each wed an extraordinary woman. In 1855, Henry married Lucy Stone, the great woman's rights and anti-slavery activist, who told him from the very outset she would never marry. He pursued her so indefatigably, however, that finally she gave up— on condition that she continue her activism and keep her own last name. (Even today, women who do not take their husband's names in marriage are called "Lucy Stoners.")

Within a year of Henry's marriage, Sam wed Lucy's best friend, Antoinette Brown. The women had met at Oberlin College, where they both earned degrees. This was an extraordinary achievement in an era when women were not supposed to go to college. Both were interested in woman's rights, but Antoinette's deepest passion was religion; and just as Elizabeth had set her sights on medicine, so Nettie had set hers on the ministry, to become the first woman minister ordained in America.

In the fall of 1856, Sam and his wife moved into Elizabeth's house in New York, where Nettie promptly gave birth—assisted by Dr. Blackwell—to Dr. Blackwell's first niece, Florence. By that time, the household in Manhattan was complete. The family hardware business out in Cincinnati had been sold. Along with Sam and Nettie, now Henry, Lucy, Mama, and Marian moved east to New York City. Fifteen carts of furniture accompanied them. Then from Cleveland came Marie Zakrzewska, M.D. And from across the sea came Dr. Emily Blackwell.

For one fleeting moment, the majority of the Blackwells lived together again, beneath one roof, and beneath that roof there were three women doctors.

Now seemed the time to launch a full-fledged hospital, staffed entirely by women, along the lines Elizabeth had fantasized with Florence Nightingale, and Zak and Emily. As early as 1852, Elizabeth had written, "I hope some day to arrange a hospital on truer principles than any that we have yet seen. . . . A center of Science, and of moral growth, . . . my Hospital [would] cure my patients spiritually as well as physically, and what innumerable aids that would necessitate! I must have the church, the school, the workshop . . . to cure my patients—a whole society, in fact."

Her hospital's founding seemed all the more pressing because of two recent developments on the local medical scene.

A leading specialist in women's diseases, Dr. J. Marian Sims, had recently come north to open the New York Woman's Hospital for the treatment of female diseases. The most conservative doctors (and their wives) supported him—those who were dead set against allowing women to practice medicine. Dr. Sims made a point of being impeccably polite to Emily and Elizabeth Blackwell. Indeed, they had high hopes of working hand-in-hand with him when he first appeared. But never, ever, did he stoop to having any professional dealings with them. His new hospital represented a major conservative effort to keep women patients away from women doctors.

The second pressing reason to found her hospital now, as Elizabeth saw it, was that eight female students at a hydropathic institute in the city had recently won permission to attend clinical lectures and visits at New York Hospital. Since it was the first time women had been given this opportunity, she found the gesture encouraging, but she was alarmed that these young ladies were water curists, not regular physicians. Among other things, she feared that they might disgrace themselves by their lack of medical knowledge, thereby blackening the name of all women physicians.

Elizabeth's growing sense of urgency was shared by Emily and Zak. But practical Zak advised that they not aim too high at first. Start small and soon, said Zak, just as you did with your dispensary. Then raise more money and expand.

This seemed an excellent plan, but when the three physicians started telling people they might open a small hospital run entirely by women, they were greeted with the same response Elizabeth had gotten at every stage of her career: *It can't be done.* They were told, as she reported: "that female doctors would be looked upon with so much suspicion that the police would interfere; that if deaths occurred their death certificates would not be recognized; that they would be resorted to by classes and persons whom it would be an insult to be called upon to deal with; that without men as resident physicians they would not be able to control the patients; . . . and, finally, that they would never be able to collect money enough for so unpopular an effort."

Elizabeth, Emily, and Zak refused to dwell on dismal predictions. They would rent a house and raise sufficient money dime by dime, if necessary. Zak proposed that they ask the abolitionist women who had been organizing against slavery for years how they managed to raise their funds. Let us copy the experts, Zak said. And she set out for Boston to find the answer

She came back shortly with $650 in contributions and the suggestion that they hold a large crafts fair to benefit their hospital. This they did in mid-December, 1856, in the dilapidated attic of the Stuyvesant Institute, no other quarters being offered by anyone for so radical a cause. Horace Greeley's *Tribune* announced that they had made "over $1,100 from sales and money donations." Their goal was $5,000. And so back to Boston went Zak, to return to New York with another $650 and the promise of that amount again each year for two years to come. It was enough to rent an old Dutch house at 64 Bleecker Street.

On May 12, 1857, the New York Infirmary for Indigent Women and Children opened its doors. The Blackwells had selected this date—Florence Nightingale's birthday—in tribute to her as an old and valued friend who had transformed the nursing profession. Many members of the Anti-Slavery Society, the Temperance Union, and the Home Missionary Society, among other socially conscious organizations, came to the Infirmary's grand opening. The Reverend Henry Ward Beecher spoke, and Elizabeth, dressed in her white doctoral sack, presented a report. Then she invited everybody present to inspect the new premises.

The building fronted on Bleecker Street, which was highly respectable and served as an entrance to the hospital. But the back of the house faced tenements as overcrowded and disease-ridden as anyone could wish. It was a perfect location. The hospital would charge patients who could afford it four dollars a week; all others would be treated free. The budget for one week came to twenty-two dollars. This covered food, wages, heat, and lighting.

The outpatient dispensary was on the first floor, where front and back parlors had been combined to form one large room. The second floor contained two six-bed wards. The whole of the third floor was given over to maternity, except for a little hall which became the doctors' sitting room. On the fourth floor was living space for the medical staff and servants. The Doctors Blackwell slept at Elizabeth's house on 15th Street, but Dr. Zak moved to the infirmary and became the resident physician. One small bedroom had been turned into an operating room and it, like all the other rooms in the hospital, was heated by an open coal grate fire. Since they could not afford to buy furniture, the doctors had accepted any items offered—weary brocaded sofas, balding velvet hourglass chairs, the humblest of tables, the least elegant of shelves and stools.

The German and Irish immigrants who flocked to the infirmary did not seem to mind. Between May, 1857, and January, 1858, the doctors treated 866 cases, hospitalizing forty-eight. In the infirmary's second year, the patient load doubled. Elizabeth served as director, Emily was in charge of surgery, and Zak specialized in medicine. Soon the doctors were joined by five medical students from female medical schools in Philadelphia and Boston. Thus the staff was entirely female, although Elizabeth had managed to attract a number of eminent male doctors to the board of consulting physicians, who thereby gave official male sanction to the institution.

The New York Infirmary was a success.

Not that there were no difficult moments in its early days. Early on, a young woman died in childbirth. Word of her death got out, and within hours the news had spread like wildfire through the neighborhood that the lady doctors were killing their patients.

Led by the grief-stricken, angered members of the

dead woman's family, an unruly crowd gathered outside the infirmary doors. They hooted and yelled. Soon, they filled the street. Some brandished pickaxes and shovels. They rattled them against the cobblestones. Their mood grew more inflamed, until somebody shouted, "Push down the doors!"

The mob surged forward. Trapped inside, the doctors tried to calm their terrified patients.

Then, suddenly, two young policemen pushed their way through to the front of the crowd. Get back! they yelled.

These two had frequently escorted the lady doctors home at night and had become their self-appointed guardians. Now they reasoned with the crowd. No doctor could possibly keep every single patient from dying, they said.

Slowly, gradually, the tension outside eased. And finally the crowd dispersed.

A similar scene occurred a few months later, when a patient died of a ruptured appendix. Then, sometime after that, a fire raged through the livery stables in back, threatening to engulf the hospital. All the nurses were dispatched to wet down the infirmary roof. As the horses next door broke through the flames and fled into the streets in panic, the doctors struggled to restrain their patients from doing the exact same thing.

These early incidents receded gradually into the background, though, and, slowly, season upon season and year after year, the Doctors Blackwell and Zakrzewska won the trust of their neighborhood and fame far beyond it. They had put down roots.

Their accomplishment was all the more impressive in that, throughout their early years, the country as a whole was spinning into a severe financial crisis yet again. Banks and businesses were going under, just as they had done in 1837, pushing Samuel Blackwell west to Cincinnati. Now, in 1857, the year his daughters launched their hospital, there were more than thirty thousand jobless in New York City alone, and the infirmary's finances, just like everybody else's, were in trouble.

As director, Elizabeth was forced continuously to seek funds, by any and all means—private donations, charity bazaars, benefit concerts, and lectures for which fees were charged. Openly in search of donors, Dr. Blackwell cultivated likely circles of New York society, especially those known for philanthropy. She and sometimes Zak and sometimes even Emily appeared, after a very long day's work, at soirees and salons all over Manhattan to try to woo the wealthy and the idealistic to their cause.

One day, they learned that the great Shakespearean actress Fanny Kemble was performing in the city. They knew she occasionally did benefits for the causes she supported. Since Elizabeth had met her once in England, she tucked Zak's arm beneath her own and went to pay a call.

The famous actress received her visitors with courtesy. They chatted politely for a while.

Then Elizabeth brought up the object of their visit.

You are interested, are you not, in forward-looking causes? she asked.

Indeed, said Fanny Kemble.

Elizabeth spoke about the founding of the New York

Infirmary for Indigent Women and Children. In moving detail, Zak described the population that it served.

Their hostess listened with interest.

The doctors invoked the desperate financial situation of the hospital. They wondered if Miss Kemble might consider doing a benefit reading.

The actress nodded sympathetically.

We are, after all, an historic institution, said Elizabeth. There is no other hospital where all the physicians are women.

At that revelation, Fanny Kemble "sprang up to her full height," Elizabeth wrote, "turned her flashing eyes upon us, and with the deepest tragic tones of her magnificent voice exclaimed:

'Trust a woman—as a *doctor?! Never!*'"

Chapter Fifteen

Barbara Leigh Smith, Elizabeth's old friend from England, had come to New York City for a visit. After applauding the new hospital, Barbara urged Elizabeth to train her sights on her real home—England.

We are so backward, Barbara said. There are no British women doctors yet, let alone hospitals staffed entirely by women. We need your genius, your leadership.

Elizabeth listened with her heart. She had not wanted to leave London in 1851. She had always planned to go back. This was perhaps the moment. Surely Emily and Zak could manage the hospital for a year without her. During that year, she might explore the possibility of founding a London infirmary for women and children.

But Elizabeth had another ambition in mind, as well.

Barbara told her that the British medical profession was determined, for the first time, to enforce uniform standards among physicians throughout the United Kingdom. A General Council of Medical Education and Registration had been formed that would publish a Medical Registry. Only doctors in the registry would be allowed to practice in the United Kingdom. But doctors with foreign degrees would be eligible to register, too, if they were practicing medicine in England before October 1, 1858.

Elizabeth's pulse quickened. If she could open a British practice now, she stood a chance of being registered. Then at least one woman physician would exist, officially, on record in the United Kingdom. It was just the sort of tangible prize and the kind of measurable proof of women's progress that Elizabeth loved to claim.

She announced her decision to return to England.

Perhaps her excitement blinded her. Or perhaps the unwavering focus she was so famous for got in her way. Whatever the case, as she made plans to leave for England, she did not see what was happening in her own backyard.

Dr. Emily Blackwell, after years of single-minded dedication, had decided she was in the wrong profession. Emily wrote in her journal in July 1858: "A terrible trial has fallen upon me. An agony of doubt has burnt in my heart for months. Oh my God, is the end of all my aspirations, of my prayers and dreams, to be that this long earnest struggle has been a mistake, that this life of a Physician is so utterly not my life that I can not express myself through it—and worse—worse—that I might have done more in other ways. Oh my Father Thou who seest how pure and true were my motives, leave me not . . . I could bear anything but the feeling of failure, show me the way, be with me!"

Emily hid her turmoil from Elizabeth. What good would it do to tell her? The very thought of saying to her sister *I don't think I want to be a doctor* took Emily's breath away. How could she speak these words, after so much struggle, to Elizabeth Blackwell, M.D.? Her older sister counted on her. For the moment, Emily was stuck. She said nothing.

Oblivious to Emily's pain, Elizabeth sailed for England in August, taking with her the eleven-year-old Kitty. Elizabeth's brother Howie met their boat and escorted them to London, where Elizabeth enrolled Kitty in an experimental boarding school for boys and girls that Barbara had said was in the vanguard of reform. With Kitty in school, Elizabeth visited as many old friends as she could in London, then moved on to Paris.

There, she settled down for a prolonged visit with her sister Anna, whom she had not seen for seven years. Anna was working as foreign correspondent to a number of American newspapers, and she had promised her sister the space and quiet Elizabeth would need to compose a series of lectures she had been invited to give in cities all over England. These were to examine the principles of health and disease prevention and the advantages and means of opening the medical profession to women.

As she worked, Elizabeth could not know that Kitty was miserable in her boarding school or that all the children's letters to the outside world were censored. Kitty had not lived with Her Doctor for four years, however, without learning to resist. After careful thought, she managed to slide a stamp, unseen, into her pocket. Then she quietly wrote a secret letter, which she carried with her everywhere she went, until there came a moment, on the walk she and her fellow students took each afternoon, when she could smuggle it into the mail. As soon as it arrived, her Uncle Howie showed up at the schoolhouse door to rescue her.

Like the heroine in a fairy tale, she was transported to the flat that Howie shared with his sister Ellen. There, Kitty spent the rest of the year.

As for Elizabeth, that year in Europe brimmed with what she called her "pioneer work." In 1859, she succeeded in becoming the first woman doctor officially inscribed in the British Medical Registry. She also delivered her lectures on women and medicine in London, Manchester, Birmingham, and Liverpool to great acclaim. On at least one occasion, a woman in the front row was so moved that she wept throughout Elizabeth's talk.

What Dr. Blackwell was not successful at was raising enough money to launch a women's hospital in London. This was a disappointment, but she did not take it as final. In the summer of 1859, she returned to New York City, for she was needed there. But she vowed, as she had seven years before, to return to her native land someday to carry on her work.

The New York Infirmary was thriving. In her absence, its trustees had decided to raise fifty thousand dollars to buy a permanent site where, in addition to the hospital itself, they could establish a women's medical college and a school of nursing.

Elizabeth plunged into fundraising as soon as she got back, and by January, 1860, there was enough money to purchase a house at 126 Second Avenue. There, the Doctors Blackwell set up the infirmary and, convinced that it made sense to live and work in the same place, they themselves moved in. They continued to eat in the basement and sleep up under the roof, as they had in the house on 15th Street; but here they shared the building with their patients rather than with boarders. If their frugal use of space had not changed, though, other things most certainly had.

Zak was gone. She had left for the New England Female Medical College in Boston to become professor of obstetrics and diseases of women and children.

Even before her departure, Zak had taken to having sudden headaches whenever she felt too much was being asked of her, which it quite frequently was, during Elizabeth's absence. But too much work alone had not sent her away. When Dr. Blackwell had first undertaken to help her, Zak had promised her two years of service. This Zak had fulfilled. At the end of those two years, she needed to be on her own. And she had other reasons, too, for leaving the New York Infirmary. Zak had grown impatient with what she called the Blackwells' negativity. They were always finding fault, she said. Even in moments of great triumph, they could not or would not allow themselves to experience joy. Zak's spunky spirit differed from theirs. She never underestimated their accomplishments nor her own gratitude. But she was ready for a change.

Zak's departure was not the most wrenching disappointment Elizabeth faced when she came home from England. For it was then that Emily confessed her secret. She had made a terrible mistake, she said. She was not meant to be a doctor after all. The minute that she could, she would quit medicine completely.

Elizabeth was bitterly disappointed. No wonder her

eye inflammation flared up at this time, rendering her incapable of reading for weeks.

"Emily's determination is to leave the profession," she wrote to her friend Barbara in England. "She has taken an extreme dislike to it, and though she performs her duties conscientiously, she only does in medicine what is unavoidable & no longer studies with any future object. Anything like a position in Surgery, is therefore out of the question, and she will never practise in England—when she has collected a small competency [income to live on], she will travel and devote herself to art . . . I used what influence I could at first, but the subject is now never discussed by us—it will at any rate be years before she is in a position to carry out her plans."

Emily was terribly unhappy. Elizabeth was restless and deeply disillusioned. But they were bound to one another and to their hospital. There was not enough money for Emily to leave medicine nor for Elizabeth to return to London. For the time being, the Doctors Blackwell were obliged to stay right where they were.

They moved together into the new infirmary, setting up its departments as they had in their previous hospital and dispensary, and instituting a new position on the medical staff: sanitary visitor.

"This post," wrote Elizabeth, "was filled by one of our assistant physicians, whose special duty it was to give simple, practical instruction to poor mothers on the management of infants and the preservation of the health of their families."

The sanitary visitor went into ill-ventilated, over-crowded, disease-ridden tenements to help her clients improve their living conditions. She opened windows, distributed soap and clean linens, and preached the importance of cleanliness, diet, sun, and exercise. She left pamphlets, written in whatever language was spoken by the family, which discussed hygiene and health. A step toward what is now called social work, her job was an important innovation.

In 1860, Elizabeth and Emily began to make concrete plans to open a medical school. Both doctors had reservations about its being an all-women's college, but their course was dictated by the obstacles they met. Elizabeth had not wanted to study at La Maternité, but no other medical facility would let her in. She had not wanted to found her own New York dispensary, but all the existing hospitals had closed their doors to her. It was not her original plan to found an all-woman hospital, but women doctors were shut out of clinical experience. Given women's ongoing exclusion from regular medical education and the low standards (in Elizabeth's view) of existing female medical schools, she felt that the Blackwells must open their own medical college for women. Emily agreed.

The two began to solicit students and funds. Elizabeth lectured on "medicine as a profession for women" and on the necessity of a four-year medical education for women. She published a "Letter to Young Ladies Desirous of Studying Medicine" in the *English Woman's Journal,* hoping to attract British students. Everything she said and wrote stressed the importance of clinical experience and of the "highest professional standards" in women's medical studies.

Then, suddenly, the world came to a halt. On April 12, 1861, in Charleston, South Carolina, where Elizabeth had lived, taught, and read medicine for a year and a half, Confederate soldiers fired upon Fort Sumter. The American Civil War had begun.

The Blackwells had fought slavery from their earliest youth. "To us," Elizabeth wrote, "nourished from childhood on the idea of human freedom and justice, the contest became of absorbing interest. . . . We threw ourselves energetically into the cause of freedom."

Before the end of April, the sisters called an informal meeting at the infirmary to discuss the training of women nurses for the wounded. When an announcement of the meeting inadvertently appeared in the *New York Times,* hundreds of women packed the infirmary to overflowing. A second meeting was called in a bigger space to which three thousand women came. There, the Woman's Central Association of Relief was formed, and Elizabeth was named chair of its Registration Committee. To Barbara in England, she wrote, "There has been a perfect mania amongst the women, to 'act Florence Nightingale'!" The crucial task of Elizabeth's committee was to screen the multitudes who wanted to become "the Lady with the Lamp."

The army in those days used only male nurses and recuperating soldiers, untrained and sick themselves, to care for its sick and wounded. Nursing was not for ladies. Just as no proper member of the "delicate sex" would consider applying to medical school, no genuine lady would volunteer to be a nurse. Any woman who did so must be a prostitute or a crazed advocate of woman's rights with an ax to grind. This the male establishment persisted in asserting, despite Florence Nightingale's much-acclaimed work. With the outbreak of the Civil War in 1861, however, America's need for nurses was desperate. And so, with the greatest reluctance and only under enormous pressure from the public, especially the female public (which was sending its husbands and brothers and sons into battle), the War Department agreed to allow women to serve. But those who did so must be exemplary, above reproach.

The Doctors Blackwell screened applicants and helped train volunteers from New York before they went to Washington for assignment. As part of the training, Elizabeth gave nine lectures on subjects ranging from sanitation and hygiene to the bandaging of surgical wounds, while Emily wrote a pamphlet that was widely used, entitled *The Selection and Training of Nurses*. But the two doctors would gladly have done more, had they been wanted. They were, quite specifically, not wanted. When the various state relief organizations were combined to become the United States Sanitary Commission, a group of well-known medical men took over its direction and staffed it largely with women volunteers.

"The Doctors would not permit us to come forward," wrote Elizabeth. "In the hospital committee . . . they declined to allow our little hospital to be represented—& they refused to have anything to do with the nurse education plan if 'the Miss Blackwells were going to engineer the matter.'"

Instead of naming Elizabeth, who was the obvious choice, to be Superintendent of Female Nurses, the medical establishment picked Dorothea Dix. She was no aggravating female doctor, but a brave reformist teacher who had come to fame before the war, working to improve the inhuman conditions in insane asylums. Both Blackwell sisters praised he character, but bemoaned her organizational abilities. She supervised her nurses, Elizabeth observed, "without a particle of system, but with intense benevolence."

At the beginning of the war, Dorothea Dix was not the only one without a particle of system. When the war broke out, the United States Army Medical Department consisted of fewer than one hundred men, and the Confederate Army Medical Department did not even exist. Regiments of soldiers marched off to war without a surgeon, or with a surgeon but no medical supplies. Frequently, when both were present, the surgeon did not know what he was doing and he was ignorant of how infections were spread. The wounded often died not of their wounds but of infections carried by the very physicians who were trying to cure them.

Many of the soldiers came from the countryside, rather than from densely populated cities, and they had never been exposed to "childhood" diseases such as measles, chicken pox, and diphtheria. This meant that they had no immunity; and amidst the crowds of men with whom they were suddenly forced into contact, they contracted these diseases by the thousand. The unsterile conditions of vaccination (re-use of needles, for example) simply spread disease and infection.

Added to this life-threatening situation was the fact that tens of thousands of soldiers lived together in conditions so unsanitary that they were worse than those in the seediest slums of New York. In military hospitals and living quarters alike, food and water were so contaminated and the lack of sanitation so extreme that more soldiers died from diseases such as typhoid and dysentery than from wounds inflicted by the enemy.

Whatever the cause, six hundred thousand men died in the Civil War.

The "Sanitary," as the United States Sanitary Commission came to be known, did help, on the northern side. It collected and distributed tinned—thus, uncontaminated—meat, fruit, and vegetables, along with blankets and other supplies. And, as well as nursing the troops, it educated them.

But the killing on the battlefields continued unabated, and here the women trained by the Doctors Blackwell and others proved themselves daily. Elizabeth wrote about one such woman: "After the battle of Gettysburg she spent two days and nights on the field of slaughter, wading with men's boots in the blood and mud, pulling out the still living bodies from the heaps of slain, binding up hideous wounds, giving a draught of water to one, placing a rough pillow under the head of another, in an enthusiasm of beneficence which triumphed equally over thought of self and horror of the hideous slaughter."

The Blackwells themselves never saw the front. They did their war work in New York City while running the infirmary full-time, and the city itself served to mirror how the war was going. Six weeks after the fighting had started, optimism prevailed. As Emily wrote to Barbara:

"The whole of [the city] is coloured by the war—all the parks are filled with rows of wooden barracks, and the streets are always resounding with military music as the regiments move in and out." People were euphoric in those early days. Death, destruction, crippling loss, and all the privations and tragedies that accompany war were not yet realities.

Two summers later, however, in 1863, the terrible face of war had become all too visible, even on the home front. At first, the government had relied on a volunteer army, but the fighting and the killing had not ended, and now more soldiers were needed to save the Union. In March, 1863, Congress passed the Enrollment Act: All able-bodied men between twenty and forty-five years of age were eligible to be drafted into military service.

The draft took effect on Saturday, July 11, 1863.

On Monday the twelfth, draft riots exploded in New York City.

At the time, Elizabeth was in New Jersey, at a house donated by a reformist friend in Paris (Madame de Noailles). News came that rioters were looting in the neighborhood of the Blackwell infirmary.

Just as thirty-two years earlier in England, her father had confronted the Bristol riots, Elizabeth now set out to confront her own. Seventeen-year-old Kitty insisted on going with her.

They made their way to the hospital on foot, through bedlam. The city's streetcars had stopped running. All the stores and houses that they passed were shuttered tight. The streets were strewn with fallen telegraph lines. In the distance, they saw crowds of white men armed with pitchforks, hammers, clubs, and guns, who surged from block to block in search of black men.

We are dying! the white mob cried. We are fighting a war to liberate the slaves, but the liberated slaves just come up here to steal our jobs!

The rioters uprooted pavingstones, heaved bricks through windows, and looted stores. They attacked the Coloured Orphan Asylum, which housed almost eight hundred black children. The mob burned the orphanage to the ground. Maddened, the rioters roamed the streets, setting upon any black people they encountered, beating them, stoning them. Blacks were shot. They were hanged from trees and lampposts.

Inside the infirmary, the wards were in a panic.

Everybody knew that the Blackwells supported abolition. And at that moment, while rioters raged in the streets, several black women were patients in the Blackwell infirmary: pregnant women who had fled north and were now awaiting the birth of their babies.

The hospital was a natural target for the rioters, and black and white patients alike were terrified. Through the windows, they could see the city burning. The doctors drew the curtains. Still, the flickering shadows of firelight leapt on the walls. It was like Bristol, all those years before. Elizabeth remembered standing on a hill at Olveston with Mama, knowing that Papa was somewhere amidst the distant devastation. Now it was she who stood at its center.

On the second night of rioting, the fires that the mob had set swept to within a block of the infirmary. The white patients demanded that the black patients be forced to leave.

We will all be killed! they clamored at their doctors.

That night, it seemed to Elizabeth that everything she had struggled for and accomplished in her life—everything she believed in—might go up in flames.

You've got to make them go! the white patients cried. We'll all be killed!

Elizabeth was a doctor and she was an abolitionist. Throughout her life, she had been repulsed by slavery. Her family had sheltered runaway slaves. They had attended anti-slavery meetings, written anti-slavery articles, passed out anti-slavery pamphlets in the towns out west. Elizabeth could not now betray her deepest values. She and Emily refused to abandon their black patients.

Throughout that long and fearful night, Elizabeth walked the wards with the other members of her staff. They talked calmly with their patients. They stood beside the beds and covered their patients' eyes so they would not see the flames. All that night, they prayed and waited for a terrible end.

But when the morning came, they were still there.

Another day of rioting ensued before the city sank back in its ashes. Then, life on the home front stumbled back to normal. Bedraggled troops marched off to war. New York was left in a shambles. But the infirmary had been spared.

Chapter Sixteen

When the war was over, life had changed, utterly.

The New York Infirmary was now treating nearly seven thousand patients per year, including outpatient and hospital cases. Now the Blackwells' chief goal was to found a medical college for women. A speech they had co-authored, which Elizabeth delivered in 1863, asserted that "the practice of medicine by women is no longer a doubtful, but a settled thing." The problem that remained to be tackled, the two doctors asserted, was the precise training that women doctors should receive and what further training they should get once out of medical school. They wrote: "Consider how women stand in this matter, how alone, how unsupported; no libraries, museums, hospitals, dispensaries, clinics; no endowments, scholarships, professorships, prizes, to stimulate and reward study; no time-honored institutions and customs, no recognized position; no societies, meetings, and professional companionship; all these things men have, none of them are open to women."

This is what we must work toward, said the Blackwells, all of this for women.

In 1865, the trustees of the New York Infirmary applied to the state legislature for a college charter and began to seek contributions once again to the college fund. Elizabeth traveled to Washington and Boston for fundraising. She lectured in New York. She wrote to European friends.

Three years later, in November 1868, the Woman's Medical College of the New York Infirmary opened its doors.

Its earliest lectures were delivered in a classroom rented from New York University, and three women served on the faculty of eight during its first year. Emily Blackwell was professor of obstetrics and diseases of women; Lucy M. Abbott was her assistant and taught clinical midwifery; and Elizabeth Blackwell was professor of hygiene, a faculty position that did not exist at other medical schools. Elizabeth was the first professor of preventive medicine in America, and she spoke of this and other innovations in her opening address at the Woman's Medical College on November 2, 1868.

All of its graduates, she said, would be required to study medicine for three years, rather than the usual two (the requirement soon became four). The college's Examining Board would be made up of physicians who were not on the faculty and who would therefore be tougher judges of the students. In later years, one of the members of the board commented: "I am now ashamed of the type of questions we required those young women to answer. I am sure no one would have tolerated them in our own colleges. But our excuse must be that Dr. Blackwell demanded more difficult questions than could be submitted to our students, for she was determined that all women graduated from her college should be a carefully selected group."

All students at the college would be expected to play an active role in their own education: they would be asked to talk about what they were learning, to "recite," not simply to listen passively while others lectured. And they would do clinical work, hands-on, not simply memorize and parrot back disembodied theory. Students at the college would be expected to *know* medicine.

Elizabeth declared: "Let us give all due weight to sympathy, and never dispense with it in the true physician; but it is knowledge, not sympathy, which can administer the right medicine. It is observation and comprehension, not sympathy, which will discover the kind of disease; and though warm sympathetic natures, with knowledge, would make the best of all physicians—without sound knowledge, they would be most unreliable and dangerous guides."

By the time the first class graduated, the Woman's Medical College had moved to its new quarters at 130 Second Avenue, down the block from the New York Infirmary. Students could do clinical work there, and by then they were permitted to work also at Bellevue Hospital, the New York Eye and Ear Infirmary, the Northern Dispensary, and the Demilt Dispensary.

But by the time the first class graduated, Elizabeth had gone home to England.

She and Emily had finally parted company—and not

without fireworks. According to Kitty, "Aunt Marian told Dr. Elizabeth that she had alienated and was alienating Aunt Emily. My Doctor wrote to Madame Bodichon [Barbara] about it and Madame Bodichon urged her to come to England and settle there." Emily was claiming her own place, refusing to be dominated by Elizabeth. They were both strong women, who had worked together to open up a field that had been closed to members of their sex. Now each Dr. Blackwell needed her own terrain. The break between them had finally come, and it was Elizabeth—not Emily—who left. And with her older sister gone, the younger Dr. Blackwell finally came into her own. She practiced medicine and ran the New York Infirmary and the Woman's Medical College brilliantly until she retired in her old age.

But Elizabeth felt she needed "to renew physical strength . . . and to enlarge my experience of life." To her friend Barbara, awaiting her eagerly on the other side of the sea, she wrote: "I am coming with the one strong purpose in my mind of assisting in the establishment, or opening of a thorough medical education for women, in England—As soon as the Doctorate is freely attainable by English women, I shall feel as if my public work—my own special pioneer mission, were over—but not until then."

On July 15, 1869, she left New York behind her, sailing out toward the Old World, a pioneer returning, to renew her quest.

Elizabeth Blackwell was forty-eight years old when she went home to England. She was no longer the little girl who had peeped through the banisters so many years before, excluded and alone. Now she had earned her place at the table, an honored guest. Like the voluble Mr. Burnet from Cork, Dr. Blackwell had her own tales to tell about the great wide world and her adventures in it.

The world had changed. It was different from what it had been. And she was one who had helped make it so.

Afterword

How far the world was from perfection still, how much still left to do!

In London Dr. Blackwell set up a medical practice and taught at the London School of Medicine for Women, established in 1874—with her active participation—by a former student, Sophia Jex-Blake.

By 1879, however, Elizabeth was in such frail health that she could no longer fight on the front lines of reform. She lectured and wrote about the world, but she could not transform it with her own unflinching, visionary presence, as she once had done. She was obliged to leave the bustle of London for a quieter place, and this was "a terrible blow," she wrote to Barbara. "[London] is where I want to live; and it throws me out of my medical plans that I cannot do so. I must therefore reshape the remainder of my life, and I am feeling my way for that purpose."

In March of 1879 she and Kitty moved to Rock House, a lovely little country house perched on a hill overlooking the English Channel at Hastings. This was where she was to spend most of the rest of her life, writing numerous articles, lectures, and books, in what was a second long and prolific career. Her first major work of the period, entitled *Counsel to Parents on the Moral Education of*

Their Children, was outspoken (for the period) in its discussion of sex education. This scandalized the British public. Elizabeth was in her element.

In addition to writing, she advised and inspired a whole generation of young British women who were trying to break into the medical field, and worked with numerous organizations (the National Health Society, the Association of Registered Medical Women, the Moral Reform Union, the Social Purity Alliance) which espoused political, social, and moral causes. She campaigned for widespread education in hygiene and against legalized prostitution; she participated in local politics, and was in fact the first Blackwell woman ever to cast a vote; she took up causes like antivivisectionism—that is, opposition to the use of animals in scientific experiments.

This is one of the issues on which scientists who came after her questioned the stand she took, but she had her own deeply felt reasons. She was against using animals in medical experiments not just because she loved dogs (as she did), but also because she believed that, if doctors could bring themselves to make helpless animals suffer in the name of science, they might blunt the "intelligent sympathy with suffering" that any true healer must have. She feared "the triumph of intellect over morality" in her profession, which was a way of saying that she feared the triumph of what she saw as the male attitude toward medicine (detached and technological) over the female attitude (compassionate and nurturing). She feared a loss of empathy for human beings, especially the poor and the helpless, who all too easily might become mere objects of research.

What then followed, logically, were experiments—or, at the very least, unnecessary operations—on humans. Women, she feared, were especially vulnerable targets. Indeed, the late nineteenth century saw the development of an operation called an "ovariotomy," the removal of a woman's ovaries, which surgeons began to perform routinely as a cure for many "women's complaints," from cramps to insanity. Ovariotomies became as common in Elizabeth's time as mastectomies and hysterectomies have become in ours. She adamantly opposed them. For somewhat similar reasons, she opposed the new discoveries being made in bacteriology, chiefly, the germ theory of disease. If doctors located the cause of disease in germs, she worried, might they not stop treating the patient and start treating the disease instead? Might they not lose sight altogether of the human being for whom they were caring? Elizabeth believed physicians must treat each patient holistically, seeing each as an individual, rooted in a specific environment, a specific life, and possessing not just a body but also a mind and a soul.

It turned out that Dr. Blackwell's indignant rejection of the germ theory was misguided, but in her holistic approach to patients, as in her antivivisectionism, she anticipated some of the major questions raised by late-twentieth century medicine: have we lost sight of the suffering human creature in our rush toward ever more advanced medical technology? Is it really always best to perform intricate, painful, expensive procedures that leave patients technically alive but terribly impaired? Is it really always preferable to attach the sick to machines that breathe and eat for them, instead of allowing them to die?

Does today's astounding technology represent what Elizabeth would call the triumph of intellect over morality? For her, it was women physicians, in particular, who must insure the higher morality of medicine. On optimistic days, she believed that her female colleagues united "the physician of the body and the physician of the soul."

But on darker days, especially toward the end of her life, she worried that women doctors were simply buying into the male system. "The only disappointment which comes to me now," she wrote, "as I draw towards the close of a life full of joy and gratitude is the surprise with which I recognise that our women physicians do not all and always see the glorious moral mission, which as women physicians they are called on to fulfill. It is not by simply following the lead of male physicians, and imitating their practices, that any new and vitalizing force will be brought into the profession."

Elizabeth expected more of women than she did of men, and during her last years she saw the ranks of women doctors swell, despite the ongoing efforts of the medical establishment to exclude them. Throughout the late 1800's, male physicians were still making speeches about how it was their professional duty to "redeem woman from the bondage of her education and restore her to wifehood and motherhood; to uplift the sexual conscience of the community; . . . and to fill our homes with prattling children." This was the doctor's great mission, "which he must cheerfully and manfully accept as his Duty of the Hour."

But progress continued despite such reactionary sentiments. Thus, for instance, when the medical college at

Johns Hopkins University opened in 1893, it was coeducational. This fact represented a triumph, won by a small group of woman's rights advocates who also happened to be the organizers of Bryn Mawr College: M. Carey Thomas, Mary Garrett, Elizabeth King, and Mary Gwinn.

When Johns Hopkins announced that it wished to open a medical school but lacked the money to do so, these women raised $100,000 and offered it to the university, with the proviso that women be permitted to study medicine. The administrators and trustees did not like this idea any more than had their forebears at Geneva Medical College; and just like them, they invented a foolproof way out: they promised to accede to their donors' wishes, if the enormous sum of $500,000 could be raised.

Their scheme, like the Geneva scheme, backfired. When a national campaign raised only $200,000, one of the four women, Mary Garrett, contributed $300,000 of her own. The agreed-upon sum was met. The trustees had made a bargain. Women students were thus admitted to the Johns Hopkins Medical School.

That was a hundred years ago. The late nineteenth century was a splendid era for women in medicine, who entered the profession by the thousands. But during the first half of the twentieth century, caught in a violent backlash, the percentage of women doctors declined sharply. It took the second wave of feminism, during the 1960's, to reverse the trend again. Now, at the end of the twentieth century, nearly 50% of the students enrolled in American medical schools are women.

Elizabeth celebrated her spiritual sisters' triumph at Johns Hopkins, although she no longer lived in the

United States. She was to see her adoptive country one more time before her death. In 1906, she revisited America, on the occasion of her sister Emily's eightieth birthday.

By that time five of their siblings had died: Howard, Marian, Anna, Ellen, and Sam. Then, back home in England, in 1907, she herself suffered a bad fall, from which she never fully recovered. She "lost some of her powers of concentration," as Kitty said. So much so that when Henry died in 1909, it was not clear that Elizabeth even understood he was gone.

Eight months later, on May 31, 1910, it was her turn. Her obituary in the *London Times* read, in part: "She was in the fullest sense of the word a pioneer who, like all pioneers (when discouraged) heard but did not listen."

Kitty buried Her Doctor in Scotland, at Kilmun, overlooking Holy Loch, where the two of them had spent many summers together, amidst the Scottish hills. At Rock House, in Hastings, a plaque was put up, celebrating Elizabeth. On it were inscribed these verses by Robert Browning, in which only the gender was revised:

One who never turned her back but marched breast forward,
Never doubted clouds would break,
Never dreamed, though rights were worsted, wrong would
    triumph,
Held we fall to rise, are baffled to fight better,
Sleep to wake.

Chronology of Elizabeth Blackwells' Life

1821	Elizabeth Blackwell is born in Bristol, England on February 3.
1832	She and her family immigrate to America. They settle in New York City.
1838	Elizabeth and her family move to Cincinnati, Ohio (May).
1838	Elizabeth's father dies (August). The impoverished Blackwell women start a school. Elizabeth teaches in it for six years.
1844	She opens a new school in Henderson, Kentucky.
1845	Her "moral crusade" to become a doctor begins in Ashville, North Carolina, where she teaches, saves money, and reads medicine.
1846	She teaches in Charleston, South Carolina, and she studies medicine with Dr. Samuel H. Dickson.
1847	Elizabeth applies to medical schools 29 times (May–October).
1847	Elizabeth is accepted and enrolls at Geneva Medical College.
1849	She lives and studies at La Maternité in Paris, France (June–October).
1849	She catches an eye infection from one of her patients (November).
1850	She loses her left eye (August). She moves to London to study at St. Bartholomew's Hospital (October).
1851	She sets up medical practice in New York City (September).
1852	She lectures on and publishes *The Laws of Life with Special Reference to the Physical Education of Girls* (March). Her practice grows.
1853	She opens a small dispensary (March).

1854 She incorporates The New York Dispensary for Poor Women and Children, and meets the future doctor Marie Zakrzewska. Emily Blackwell earns her M.D. Kitty Barry comes to live with Elizabeth.

1857 Elizabeth, Emily, and Zak found the New York Infirmary for Indigent Women and Children (May).

1858–59 Elizabeth spends a year in England, where she becomes the first woman to be listed in the British Medical Registry.

1861–65 During the American Civil War, Elizabeth and Emily train women nurses in New York City.

1868 Elizabeth and Emily found the Woman's Medical College of the New York Infirmary (November). Elizabeth is Professor of Hygiene.

1869 Elizabeth moves back to England permanently (June). There, she helps open the medical profession to women and writes on moral reform.

1910 Elizabeth Blackwell dies in Hastings, England on May 31, at the age of 89.

Selected Bibliography

Abram, Ruth J. *Women Doctors in America, 1835-1920*. New York: W. W. Norton & Company, 1985.

Anderson, Romola & R.C. *The Sailing Ship*. New York: Robert M. McBride & Company, 1947.

Baker, Rachel. *The First Woman Doctor*. New York: Julian Messner, Inc., 1944.

Benton, Barbara. *Ellis Island. A Pictorial History*. New York: Facts on File, Inc., 1987.

Blackwell, Elizabeth. *Essays in Medical Sociology*. London: Bell, 1902.

_____ . Letters to Barbara Bodichon. Butler Library, Columbia University Collection.

_____ . *Medicine and Morality*. London: Social Purity Alliance, undated.

_____ . *The Moral Education of the Young*. New York: Scribner, 1898.

_____ . *Pioneer Work in Opening the Medical Profession to Women*. London: Longmans, Green and Co., 1895.

Chambers, Peggy. *A Doctor Alone*. London: The Bodley Head, 1956.

Cott, Nancy F. *The Bonds of Womanhood: "Woman's Sphere" in New England, 1780-1835*. New Haven: Yale University Press, 1977.

Cross, Barbara, ed. *The Educated Woman in America*. New York: Teachers College Press, 1965.

Duffy, John. *The Healers: A History of American Medicine*. Urbana, Illinois: University of Illinois Press, 1979.

Emerson, Ralph Waldo. *Complete Works, Volume I: Nature, Addresses, and Lectures*. Boston: Houghton, Mifflin and Company, 1890.

Fancourt, Mary St. J. *They Dared To Be Doctors.* London: Longmans, Green and Co., 1965.

Hays, Elinor Rice. *Morning Star: A Biography of Lucy Stone.* New York: Harcourt, Brace & World, Inc., 1961.

_____ . *Those Extraordinary Blackwells.* New York: Harcourt, Brace & World, Inc., 1967.

Jex-Blake, Sophia. *Medical Women.* Edinburgh: Oliphant, 1886.

Kolodny, Annette. *The Land Before Her.* Chapel Hill, North Carolina: University of North Carolina Press, 1984.

Kouwenhoven, John A. *Adventures of America, 1857-1900.* New York: Harper & Brothers, 1938.

Leavitt, Judith Walzer, and Ronald L. Numbers, eds. *Sickness and Health in America.* Madison, Wisconsin: University of Wisconsin Press, 1985.

Leavitt, Judith Walzer, ed. *Women and Health in America.* Madison, Wisconsin: University of Wisconsin Press, 1984.

Lyon, Jane D. *Clipper Ships and Captains.* New York: American Heritage Publishing Co., Inc., 1962.

Marcus, Steven. *The Other Victorians.* New York: Basic Books, Inc., 1964.

Marks, Geoffrey, and William K. Beatty. *Women in White.* New York: Charles Scribner's Sons, 1972.

McCausland, Elizabeth. *American Processional.* Washington, D.C.: The Corcoran Gallery of Art, 1950.

Monteiro, Lois A. "Florence Nightingale on Public Health," *American Journal of Public Health* 75:2, 1985.

Morantz-Sanchez, Regina Markell. *Sympathy and Science.* New York: Oxford University Press, 1985.

Rosenberg, Charles & Carroll Smith-Rosenberg. "The Female Animal: Medical and Biological Views of Woman and Her Role in 19th Century America," *Journal of American History* 60 (September 1973).

Ross, Ishbel. *Child of Destiny.* New York: Harper & Brothers, 1949.

Sahli, Nancy Ann. *Elizabeth Blackwell, M.D.* New York: Arno Press, 1982.

Saxton, Martha. *Louisa May.* Boston: Houghton Mifflin, 1977.

Schlesinger, Arthur M., Jr. *The Age of Jackson.* New York: Book Find Club, 1945.

Shryock, Richard Harrison. *Medicine in America.* Baltimore: The Johns Hopkins Press, 1966.

Smith-Rosenberg, Carroll. *Disorderly Conduct: Visions of Gender in Victorian America.* New York: Oxford University Press, 1985.

Walsh, Mary Roth. *"Doctors Wanted: No Women Need Apply."* New Haven: Yale University Press, 1977.

Wellman, Paul I. *The House Divides.* New York: Doubleday & Company, 1966.

Whittier, Isabel. *Dr. Elizabeth Blackwell: The First Woman Doctor.* Brunswick, Maine: The Brunswick Publishing Co., 1961.

Wilson, Dorothy Clarke. *Lone Woman.* Boston: Little, Brown and Company, 1970.

Manuscripts and Special Collections

Academy of Medicine

Schlesinger Library on the History of Women in America, Radcliffe College

Boston Public Library

Bristol, England, City Archives

Bristol, England, Public LIbrary

British Museum

Butler Library, Columbia University

Columbia University Medical Library

Hastings, England, Public Library

Library of Congress

New York Downtown Hospital

New York Historical Society

St. Bartholomew's Hospital Archives, London

Index

THE BARNARD BIOGRAPHY SERIES

The Barnard Biography Series expands the universe of heroic women with these profiles. The details of each woman's life may vary, but each was led by a bold spirit and an active intellect to engage her particular world. All have left inspiring legacies that are captured in these biographies.

Barnard College is a selective, independent liberal arts college for women affiliated with Columbia University and located in New York City. Founded in 1889, it was among the pioneers in the crusade to make higher education available to young women. Over the years, its alumnae have become leaders in the fields of public affairs, the arts, literature, and science. Barnard's enduring mission is to provide an environment conducive to inquiry, learning, and expression while also fostering women's abilities, interests, and concerns.

Other titles in *The Barnard Biography Series:*

Beryl Markham: Never Turn Back